The Sharpest Fight

M ICHAEL AYRTON was commissioned into the Royal Corps of Signals. He instructed at the RMA Sandhurst and subsequently commanded a regular regiment in Germany. For a number of years he was responsible for the Pegasus Bridge Museum at Bénouville in Normandy. He has written a short history of Airborne Signals and is a member of the Military Historical Society and an Associate of the Royal Historical Society. He lives in South West France.

J OHN TAYLOR was commissioned into the Rifle Brigade, the successor Regiment of the 95th Rifles, and later commanded a Royal Green Jackets battalion in Hong Kong and the UK. He taught at the Army Staff College and helped to develop war gaming techniques in support of operational training. He has edited a Great War personal journal and is a member of the Society for Army Historical Research. He lives in London.

Tarbes from the Orleix Ridge
'[Tarbes] looked delightful from the heights, surrounded as it was with avenues and gardens, and backed by the lofty Pyrenees.' Blakiston

The Sharpest Fight

The 95th Rifles At Tarbes
20th March 1814

Michael Ayrton and John Taylor

forbitou

Published by Forbitou Books
PO BOX 55441
London SW4 9XW

A CIP Record for this book is available from
The British Cataloguing-in-Publication Data Office

ISBN 978-0-9554860-0-5

Design by Etica Press
Additional graphics design by Les Presses de Gascogne
Printed by Antony Rowe Ltd, Eastbourne

To the Memory
of

Captain John Duncan

2nd Battalion, 95th Rifles

and

of those Allied and French officers and men
who fell at or near Tarbes on
20th March 1814

Contents

Illustrations

Appendices

The illustrations on pages 6, 9, 13, 14, and 33 are by courtesy of the
Parker Gallery. Those on pages 39, 44, 59, 78, 121, and 136 are by
courtesy of the Royal Green Jackets Museum. The illustration on
page 42 is of reproduction weapons by courtesy of 42nd and 95th
Regts (Australia). Unless otherwise stated in the caption, all other
illustrations are from the authors' collections.

Maps

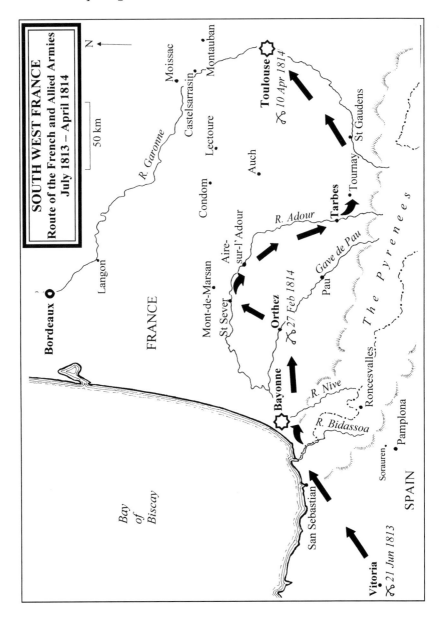

SOUTH WEST FRANCE

Route of the French and Allied Armies
July 1813 – April 1814

N

50 km

Bordeaux

R. Garonne

Langon

Moissac

Castelsarrasin

Montauban

Condom

Lectoure

Auch

Toulouse
✗ 10 Apr 1814

St Gaudens

Tournay

Tarbes

R. Adour

Gave de Pau

Pau

Aire-
sur-l'Adour

St Sever

Mont-de-Marsan

FRANCE

Orthez
✗ 27 Feb 1814

The   P y r e n e e s

Bayonne

R. Nive

Roncesvalles

Pamplona

R. Bidassoa

Sorauren

San Sebastian

SPAIN

*Bay
of
Biscay*

Vitoria
✗ 21 Jun 1813

Preface

There are now few aspects of Wellington's Peninsular Campaign that have not already been scrutinized and narrated in full. It is, therefore, all the more surprising that the detail and significance of the so-called 'Battle of Tarbes' appear to have slipped through the historians' net. It was, however, this very omission which eventually led the authors to research 'Tarbes' and, in particular, to turn the spotlight onto the action of the 95th Rifles.

John Taylor, a retired Royal Green Jackets officer, has a special interest in the subject principally because the 95th is an antecedent regiment of the Royal Green Jackets, now part of a new larger regiment, The Rifles. Michael Ayrton, also a retired army officer and living near Tarbes, has a particular interest in all aspects of Wellington's campaign in South West France. It was their mutual curiosity which initially prompted the authors to walk the battlefield in much the same way as they had walked battlefields elsewhere when they were students at the Army Staff College.

In the process of preparing for their battlefield investigation, it became apparent that the action at Tarbes on the 20th March 1814 barely achieved a mention in the principal and established histories of the Peninsular War. Many of the references were little more than thumbnail sketches whilst others were contradictory. It was not possible from these sources either to understand fully the sequence of events or to pinpoint the site of the 95th Rifles action. Nevertheless, it was decided to go ahead with the visit to Tarbes in spite of being less than fully prepared.

Once on the ground, it was obvious that many of the accounts were inaccurate. Timings, distances, and ground descriptions did not make sense. The narratives had not been related closely to the terrain. It was at this point, that the authors decided to investigate the whole subject more thoroughly and try to reconstruct the battle. It was also decided that written eyewitness accounts had to be the basis on which any such reconstruction would be made. Even these accounts would need to be corroborated against other indisputable facts.

Although warfare has changed almost beyond belief over the last two hundred years, many of the factors affecting soldiers on the ground are the same today as they were in 1814. New technologies have made possible the great increase in the speed and intensity of warfare. However, such elements as ground, weather, time and distance have not changed. Soldiers themselves are not that different; they need to eat, be watered, and to sleep. They still march at the same speed and only for so long and they can only carry certain loads. It was against this obvious but real background that all the evidence had to be validated. In addition, the authors felt that a structured military analysis of the facts might help clear the way to an understanding of the events of two hundred years ago. Perhaps this more soldierly approach, coupled with a realistic interpretation of existing texts, would be the best method of establishing the true nature of the battle.

As research progressed, it became apparent that the acknowledged histories had located the 95th Rifles' action on a ridge some three kilometres from where it actually took place. This error has been repeated in writing now so many times that it has almost become accepted fact. The discovery of the actual location, which in itself was something of a revelation, suddenly put all other evidence into context and the day's events started to make sense.

John Taylor undertook research in England mainly at the National Army Museum and at the Royal Green Jackets Museum and Archive at Winchester. Michael Ayrton carried out research mainly at *Les Archives Départementales des Hautes-Pyrénées* and *Les Archives Municipales* at Tarbes and at *Les Archives Départementales du Gers* at Auch. Both authors walked the ground extensively at Tarbes, Orleix, Oléac, Aureilhan, and in the general area of operations.

It is worth reflecting that the various eyewitness accounts of the Rifles' action and the taking of Tarbes that do exist were often written months or even years after the event although there are several which were written immediately after the action. The authors of such records were usually soldiers or officers at battalion or company level with little knowledge of wider issues. Also in 1814, there were few if any maps and certainly not down at regimental level and below. Commanders and staff had crude Departmental maps. The Cassini maps of the 1770's were known to have been used by Wellington and his staff but, at lower levels, knowledge of the ground was gleaned from cavalry and patrol reconnaissance reports and sketches. Written accounts were in the form of descriptions rather that accurate map references and consequently they were vague, particularly if no specific or identifiable topographical feature was involved. One patch of wood on an eight kilometre hill-line is very much the same as any other!

It must also be remembered that the action at Tarbes on the 20th March was over in 24 hours. It was relatively fast moving and there were two major and concurrent actions: the Light and 6th Divisions' action to the north-east of Tarbes near Orleix and the clearing of Tarbes itself by Hill's Column. The fog of war also played its part in confusing the events of the day. In addition, the French were in retreat and hardly disposed to recording the detail of their withdrawal in writing. In overall Peninsular War terms, the events at Tarbes were relatively minor and fleeting. Not unnaturally they are not given great weight in dispatches and other official communiqués. There was no formal set piece battle and casualties were relatively light. Consequently, there was no decisive or celebrated victory. It is understandable that by dawn on the 21st March, the events of the previous day had almost been forgotten; there were new and more pressing problems facing both Commanders-in-Chief.

It is not within the scope of this account to cover the wider political, strategic, and military aspects of Napoleon's campaign on the north-eastern borders of France. However, Tarbes would not make much sense if treated in total isolation. Chapter 1, therefore, summarizes the main events of the preceding nine months in SW France in the hope of giving sufficient background to understand how and why Wellington came to be facing Soult on that Sunday in March. Similarly, the events at Tarbes would be equally out of context without a brief résumé of the last few weeks of the Peninsular War.

This book records the findings of five years' research and offers, by way of a revised reconstruction, a more faithful and fuller account of the events at Tarbes. The reconstruction cannot be definitive because the evidence is incomplete and cannot support such a claim. Nevertheless, the authors are confident that the narrative is sufficiently cogent for any reader to form a clear picture of the day's happenings. It is also hoped that this account will encourage others to take a serious interest in this hitherto little known action. Indeed, had the outcome of the events at Tarbes been just marginally different, the history of the final phase of the Peninsular War would not be as we know it.

Michael Ayrton. Le Gers, Midi-Pyrénées

John Taylor. Clapham, London

January 2008

Acknowledgements

We are indebted to Dr Paddy Griffith for his guidance and advice. His observations and criticism of our early texts helped to focus our minds on the key issues and on the realities of Napoleonic warfare. We thank Mr Roger Perkins for the benefit of his publishing experience and for his sound advice. We also thank Mr Ian Robertson for his support and encouragement.

We are also grateful for the assistance provided by the staff of the Departments of Archives and of Printed Books at the National Army Museum, London. At Winchester, Major Ken Gray, the Curator of the Royal Green Jackets Museum, and Major Ron Cassidy, in charge of the Royal Green Jackets Archive, have both provided invaluable help. The staffs of the National Portrait Gallery and the Heinz Archive and Library were most helpful in locating portraits of Wellington's commanders.

We thank the *Conservateur* and the staff of *Les Archives Municipales de Tarbes* for valuable help. We are similarly grateful to the *Directeur* and the staff of *Les Archives Départementales des Hautes-Pyrénées* at Tarbes for their patience and outstanding help. We thank the *Directeur* and staff of the *Archives Départementales du Gers* at Auch for their kind assistance. We acknowledge the help and generosity of Monsieur Jacques Battesti, *Ajoint de Conservateur* at the *Musée Basque et de l'histoire de Bayonne*. Our thanks are given to the staff of the *Musée Historique* at Biarritz for access to the campaign memorial. We are indebted to the Mayors and inhabitants of the communes of Orleix, Oléac, and

Aureilhan for their tolerance and kindness in allowing us the freedom to roam over the battlefield area. We thank Monsieur Marc Sénépart of the *Association Lumières et Astronomie* at Oléac for his generosity and for access to the Oléac tower.

We are indebted to Mr Rory Constant for his generous permission to examine his relative's unpublished letters and for permission to quote from them. We thank Michel d'Arcangues, Marquis d'Iranda, for his kind permission in allowing the photograph of the original Château d'Arcangues to be reproduced. We also thank Henri, Marquis de Verthamon for his kind permission to quote from the unpublished manuscript *'Souvenirs de Famille'* written in 1876 by his Great-great-grandfather, Léonce, Baron de Claye. We are also grateful to Mr P. Beaven of Corporate Memory (Analysis), Ministry of Defence for his clear explanation of the issues associated with medals, clasps, and battle honours of the early 19th Century. We thank Monsieur Stéphane Rozes for help in locating a number of rare French portraits and we are indebted to Monsieur Alain Pigeard for his permission to reproduce portraits from his archive.

Finally, we thank all those individuals, too numerous to mention here, for their generosity, support, and hospitality and for making this project both feasible and enjoyable.

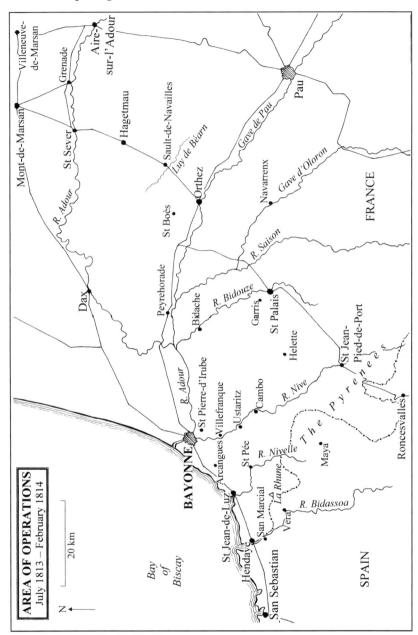

AREA OF OPERATIONS
July 1813 – February 1814

N

20 km

Bay
of
Biscay

San Sebastian

Hendaye

St Jean-de-Luz

San Marcial

Vera

Arcangues

St Pée

La Rhune

Maya

R. Nivelle

R. Bidassoa

SPAIN

BAYONNE

St Pierre-d'Irube

Villefranque

Ustaritz

Cambo

R. Nive

Helette

St Jean-
Pied-de-Port

Roncesvalles

The Pyrenees

R. Adour

Bidache

R. Bidouze

Garris

St Palais

St Boès

Peyrehorade

Dax

R. Adour

Orthez

Luy de Béarn

Sault-de-Navailles

Hagetmau

St Sever

Gave de Pau

Navarrenx

Gave d'Oloron

R. Saison

Pau

FRANCE

Aire-
sur-l'Adour

Grenade

Mont-de-Marsan

Villeneuve-
de-Marsan

I

The Pursuit into France

Some six years after the start of the so-called Peninsular War, Field Marshal Sir Arthur Wellesley, Marquess of Wellington led a combined British, Portuguese, and Spanish army from Spain across the River Bidassoa and onto French soil. The preceding campaigns in Portugal and Spain from 1807 to 1813 , from Corunna to Talavera and from Salamanca to Vitoria, were already the stuff of legend but too convoluted to summarize here.

The starting point of the Tarbes story is the summer of 1813 as the Allies manoeuvred into a position to launch their offensive from Spain into South West France. What follows here, therefore, is an outline of the twists and turns of this fascinating campaign, sub-divided into its various operational phases. Eventually, the campaign brought the Allied and French armies once more face to face but this time at Tarbes at what would turn out to be the penultimate battle of the Peninsular War.

The Situation – June and July 1813

Wellington's great victory at Vitoria on the 21st June 1813 left the Allied army poised finally to push the French out of northern Spain and back into France. Wellington had long since planned that the Allied strike against France itself should be launched from northern Spain and hit France on its border where the Pyrenees meet the Atlantic. Wellington's forces numbered some 85,000 all ranks which included

Portuguese and Spanish contingents of some 24,000 and 23,000 men respectively. He formed these into a flexible organization usually consisting of three corps, commanded by Lieutenant General Sir John Hope, Lieutenant General Sir William Carr Beresford (often given his Portuguese title of Marshal), and Lieutenant General Sir Rowland Hill. The renowned Light Division, with its three battalions of the illustrious 95th Rifles, was usually grouped in Beresford's Corps.

After Vitoria, the French in Spain were still organized into their old 'armies' of the North, Centre, and South but were demoralized. In July 1813 Napoleon appointed Maréchal Nicolas Jean de Dieu Soult, Duc de Dalmatie, to take over command of all French forces in northern Spain. Coincidentally, Soult was a native of South West France originating from St Amans-Labastide (now St Amans-Soult in the Tarn). He was ordered to arrest the deterioration of the armies' effectiveness and to ensure that neither Pamplona nor San Sebastian

Field Marshal Sir Arthur Wellesley, Marquess of Wellington.
Commander-in-Chief of the Allied Army. Engraved by Thomas Williamson after Robert Home 1812

fell to the enemy. Soult, aged 44, was an experienced general and a veteran of many campaigns in the Peninsula, and had faced Wellington and the British before. Soult straightway reorganized the various French armies into the one 'Army of Spain', which he quickly revitalized and motivated. He divided his forces into three corps each consisting of three divisions. Lieutenant général Comte Bertrand Clauzel was appointed to command the Left Wing. Lieutenant général Jean-Baptiste Drouet, Comte d'Erlon was given command of the Centre, and Lieutenant général Comte Honoré Charles Reille was to command the Right Wing. All three were experienced officers and had previously held command appointments at Army level. Soult's new Army of Spain mustered some 62,000 all ranks.

The French garrisons in Spain at San Sebastian and Pamplona had been besieged by Wellington's forces since June. These two garrisons were, in essence, now the only troops opposed to Wellington in

Maréchal Nicolas Jean de Dieu Soult, Duc de Dalmatie.
Commandant en Chef de l'Armée d'Espagne. Engraved by Lambert.

northern Spain. Although both were blockaded, the line of the western Pyrenees could not be made secure until these two garrisons had been neutralized or destroyed. San Sebastian would be needed as an Allied resupply port once the offensive against France was underway. Pamplona too, presented a problem in that it commanded the approaches to the mountain passes of Maya and Roncesvalles.

Wellington, who had been created Field Marshal after the success at Vitoria, now faced a dilemma. San Sebastian and Pamplona were some 65 kilometres distant from each other and separated by a rugged range of hills making rapid movement between the two difficult and slow. Allied forces were significantly stretched with divisions covering the Maya Pass, Roncesvalles, San Sebastian, and, in reserve, the Light and 7th Divisions.

Soult, who was at his Headquarters at Bayonne and conscious of his instructions to ensure that neither San Sebastian nor Pamplona was lost, was himself preparing an offensive to be launched from the Pyrenees. Wellington had not enough troops to block every possible approach. Nevertheless, he stood relatively well placed to redeploy his forces to meet the threat from whichever direction it materialized. It was expected that Soult would launch his offensive towards San Sebastian first.

On the 20th July 1813, Allied guns, however, opened up on San Sebastian in an attempt to breach the curtain wall. Over the next few days, further preparations for an assault were made and just before dawn on the 25th July, the storming of the breaches commenced. This brave attempt to take San Sebastian failed with heavy losses.

The Battle of the Pyrenees – July 1813

As Wellington became aware of the Allied failure at San Sebastian, he was also receiving reports of French attacks coming in from the Pyrenees at Maya and at Roncesvalles. At this stage, Wellington could not be sure if this was a French feint and that Soult's expected relief effort of the beleaguered San Sebastian was about to start. At Maya, the French nearly succeeded in pushing through and caused the Allies many casualties. In the end, the French were held. At Roncesvalles, the Allies fell back towards Pamplona but eventually established a strong defensive position at Sorauren, 6 kilometres north of Pamplona. The French delayed until reinforced which, in turn, allowed Wellington to deploy his reserves. On the 28th July, the French attacked and the next day some 25,000 men were launched against the Allied line. It was a hard fought defence and fortunately Wellington's reserves arrived just in time. The French pulled back having suffered some 4000 casualties to the Allies 2,600. Pamplona was still contained.

Next day, Soult retired westwards in the hope of coming between Wellington's forces around Pamplona and those at San Sebastian. This attempt failed. There were further clashes with the French but by the 2nd August, the French offensive evaporated and Soult ordered his somewhat disheartened troops back across the border into France. The expected direct effort to relieve San Sebastian never came but Soult's offensive certainly caught Wellington off balance and it was only just checked. At San Sebastian, the siege was once more fully reinforced and Pamplona remained blockaded. Both garrisons, however, still posed a problem which needed to be resolved.

The Fall of San Sebastian – August 1813

San Sebastian could not be starved into submission because the Allied blockade at sea was so ineffective that at night the French were able to resupply themselves by boat. The fortress would have to be stormed and, by late August, Allied breaching batteries were pounding at San Sebastians's defences. Soult, in one final attempt to save San Sebastian, launched a token two-pronged attack across the River Bidassoa at San Marcial and at Vera on the 31st August. This thrust was contained and Soult sensibly withdrew his troops back across the Bidassoa into France.

San Sebastian's defences had been pounded for five days and on the 31st August the attack was launched. The storming parties at first faltered at the breach but then, with artillery support, finally broke through. Fighting was fierce and Allied casualties heavy. The town itself was looted and virtually destroyed and on the 5th September, the remnants of the French garrison who had taken refuge in the Citadel on Monte Orgullo were ready to negotiate. On the 8th September, Général Rey surrendered the garrison and marched out of San Sebastian. He and his men were subsequently shipped back to England as prisoners. Some 3,700 casualties had been inflicted on the Allies. Meanwhile Pamplona remained blockaded by Spanish troops under the command of General Carlos D'España.

Crossing the River Bidassoa – October 1813

By October, Soult had deployed his forces defensively along the French frontier with Spain in the Pyrenees from St Jean-Pied-de-Port in the east to the Atlantic in the west. Soult anticipated that Wellington's thrust into France was most likely to come on his left and he deployed the bulk of his forces to meet that advance should it materialize. Soult did not anticipate any significant threat developing on his right around the Bidassoa estuary as the river here was a major, if not an insurmountable, obstacle.

Unbeknown to Soult however, Wellington had found a number of fordable sites in the Bidassoa estuary where, at low tide, it would be possible to cross the river. On the 6th October 1813 Wellington's troops assembled on the river's west bank south of Hendaye. Wellington had in this one sector some 24,000 Allied troops ready to attack at the very place where Soult had reasoned there was no threat. Facing Wellington in this area were a mere 4,000 French troops. At 7.25am on the 7th October 1813, the Allied 5th Division broke cover, entered the river and started to wade across. The 1st Division and the Spaniards then crossed further to the east. The French defenders

Allied troops crossing the Bidassoa.
Aquatint by J.C. Stadler after W. Heath 1813

were overwhelmed. Hendaye was quickly overrun and soon the ridge-line to the north of the river was in Allied hands. Soult had been taken by surprise and had been caught well and truly unprepared. Wellington had achieved his initial objectives within two days. His troops were now well established on the Bidassoa's east bank. Now he paused to regroup and to consider his next objectives.

Général Harispe, who was soon to join Maréchal Soult and to become a key player in the subsequent campaign against Wellington, wrote to his sister on 24th October from San-Felice. Referring to the Allied incursion into France,

> *'One has to hope that this state of affairs will not last long and that our great Emperor will not allow the English, our tough enemy, a long stay on the soil of the great Empire!'* [1]

Battle of the Nivelle – November 1813

The frontier and the dominating La Rhune mountain had been lost to the French and Soult now had to fall back and prepare another line of defence. The River Nivelle provided a perfect obstacle. The line ran from St Jean-de-Luz on the coast, along various ridge-lines, passed St Pée-sur-Nivelle and on towards St Jean-Pied-de-Port. Soult's assessment was that this time Wellington would strike on his right along the Atlantic coast sector of his defensive line. Soult, at this juncture, had some 62,000 men with 23,000 of them deployed between La Rhune and the sea. The whole line was based on an old static frontier defence system of redoubts and trenches.

Wellington, on the other hand, had some 82,000 men in total and when Pamplona capitulated on the 31st October this at last removed any French threat from the rear areas and released the Spaniards who had been besieging the town. Wellington was now poised to move again against Soult. Apart from anything else, winter was setting in and the mountains were no place for exposed troops.

As the Allied army entered France, Wellington realised that it was essential that his troops were well disciplined, respectful of property and of the French population. The retreating French army, however, caused havoc and resentment amongst the local population. French soldiers, with no pay, were tired and hungry. They were also demoralized and, now back in France, plunder was widespread. In the Allied army, Wellington imposed a regime of harsh discipline and insisted that anything and everything that was taken had to be paid for. This in turn resulted in the Allies being more welcome than the French army in their own country. It also meant that resources and provisions were denied to French troops but miraculously made available to the Allies when it was known that they could be sold and for a good profit.

Wellington moved just after dusk on the 9th November. By next day, various strong points along the French line had been captured and Soult was not able to hold the line. The Allies took St Pée-sur-Nivelle. St Jean-de-Luz had been evacuated and by that night, the French had withdrawn to a new defensive line on the River Nive which covered the approaches to the main garrison and depot town of Bayonne. The forcing of the Nivelle had cost the Allies some 2500 men with French casualties in the order of 4300.

Wellington's Spanish troops, now on French soil for the first time, resorted to looting and plunder. They were not slow to mete out to the inhabitants the sort of treatment their countrymen had received at the hands of the occupying French. This state of affairs was exactly what Wellington wished to avoid for he could not risk provoking local peasants to hostile action. Not only were the Spaniards out for revenge but they were also unpaid and left to fend for themselves by their own government. Wellington could not tolerate this situation and his Spanish contingent was ordered back into Spain. Only General Pablo Morillo's Spanish Division, which was in British pay, was saved from this humiliation

The Battle of the Nive – December 1813

Soult had now manoeuvred his divisions onto the right or east bank of the River Nive. In so doing, he hoped to canalize Wellington as he approached Bayonne between the sea and the Nive. Wellington clearly realized that to proceed towards Bayonne was dangerous unless he could force the Nive. Even so, advancing towards Bayonne either side of the river also had its hazards as the river in effect split the Allies into two elements, each unable to cross the river if needed by the other.

Wellington's army now numbered 59,000 men to Soult's 65,000. However, Soult had some 12,000 of his men in the Bayonne garrison.

On the 9th December, General Sir Rowland Hill, one of Wellington's Corps Commanders, led an Allied force of five divisions across the river between Ustaritz and Cambo. The remaining divisions of the Allied army stayed to the west of the river-line. These troops advanced towards Bayonne on a broad front. Some skirmishing took place but by the end of the day, the Allies had established a line west of the river, level with Hill on the east bank.

Lieutenant General Sir Rowland Hill.
Published by Jenkins after W. Heath 1814

Soult had, in effect, allowed the Allies to manoeuvre themselves into a dangerous position. With the Allied army divided by the River Nive, Soult now saw his chance. Under cover of night he moved four divisions from the east bank of the Nive to the west bank.

Next morning, the 10th December, Soult attacked. He had gained surprise not only in the direction of his attack but in its strength and timing. The French probed the Allied line and in places there was fierce localized fighting. The Allied line was just holding around Arcangues, defended by the Light Division who had fortified the church and chateau, but reinforcements were desperately needed. The Allies were slow to appreciate the scale and weight of the French attack. However, by 2pm reinforcements in the shape of 1st Division arrived. Allied determination had held the line, which was now reinforced, so Soult called a halt to French advances and his forces started to withdraw.

Soult's plan had been well conceived but, in the event, he had failed to deliver. He had been indecisive and had not concentrated his forces where they were needed most. The French attacking divisions, on

The Chateau at Arcangues.
Photographed in 1899 and subsequently demolished. By courtesy of Michel d'Arcangues, Marquis d'Iranda.

this occasion, had lacked spirit and their probing attacks were less than resolute. Soult had missed a rare opportunity of delivering a severe blow to Wellington who, once again, had been caught off balance by Soult and again had been lucky to escape.

The Action at St Pierre-d'Irube – December 1813

Over the next few days, after Soult's withdrawal, there was minor skirmishing and the occasional incursion but no serious challenge was made by either side. General Hill on the east of the River Nive with a force of some 14,000 men was relatively secure as a bridge had been constructed at Villefranque, providing the means of deploying troops from west to east over the river if necessary. No sooner had this pontoon bridge been built than it was washed away by a sudden spate thus leaving Hill once more isolated and vulnerable. Soult took immediate advantage and on the morning of the 13th December he launched four French divisions, with two more in reserve, against Hill's 14,000 men.

Hill's line was on the high ground with St Pierre-d'Irube in the centre. Although outnumbered, Hill's position was very strong and its narrow front caused the French difficulty in trying to deploy such a large force. The French attacked again and again but the Allied line held in spite of some fierce fighting. Hill had deployed his reserve forces to where needed most and the French momentum was lost. When the 3rd Division arrived with Wellington to support and reinforce Hill, the fight was all but over. Hill's Corps had lost some 1750 men but Soult had lost many more. Soult now retired to Bayonne but in the knowledge that the garrison there could not support his army for long. He had to break out quickly before Wellington closed the River Adour and crossed over it to the north and sealed off Bayonne. Soult accordingly deployed seven divisions on the north bank of the Adour. He moved his Headquarters to Peyrehorade and placed two divisions south of the Adour covering any approach by Wellington's right to the river.

The Push East – December 1813 to February 1814

Both sides now paused and assessed the new situation. It was mid-December and cold and wet. Roads had become impassable and resupply by pack mules was difficult and slow. Regiments and units concentrated on good husbandry and re-equipment. 1813 ended and 1814 dawned. The weather remained foul and campaigning was at a standstill. News arrived that the Austrian, Prussian, and Russian armies had crossed the Rhine and Napoleon desperately needed more troops. An obvious source was Soult's army. Soult was ordered to send two divisions with cavalry to reinforce north-eastern France and by mid-January they were en route. This sudden change to Soult's order of battle required an adjustment to French deployments around the area of Bayonne. Four divisions were now deployed south of the River Adour, two to the north and one division in Bayonne itself.

Wellington's plan was to push Soult's divisions eastwards and away from Bayonne. At the same time it was his intention to blockade Bayonne itself by crossing the Adour between Bayonne and the sea thus closing the river to the French. However, to be in a position to confront Soult's divisions and to blockade Bayonne, Wellington needed to reinforce, so he recalled some Spanish troops back from Spain. After weeks of inactivity, a general advance was ordered on the 14th February. Hill's Corps advanced towards Helette on a broad front

Lieutenant General
Sir William Carr Beresford.
Engraved by J. Rogers

while the French fell back towards the Bidouze river-line. Meanwhile the Allied 1st and 5th Divisions had been left south of Bayonne for subsequent operations in that sector.

As the French retreated towards the River Bidouze near St Palais, Général Jean Isidore Harispe, command-ing the 8th Division, decided to make a stand at Garris a few kilometres to the north-west of St Palais. Harispe had been earlier transferred from Maréchal Suchet's forces in Catalonia to Soult's command because he was a Basque with local knowledge and influence, particularly with regard to the raising of conscripts and the employment of such local forces as *Gardes Forestiers* and *Gardes Champêtres*. Wellington ordered Garris to be cleared and after fierce fighting the French withdrew in confusion over the Bidouze, blowing up the bridge as they retreated into the night. By next day, the 16th February, the bridge over the River Bidouze had been repaired. The French were in no position to hold this river-line and Soult ordered his forces to regroup on the line of the Gave d'Oloron between Peyrehorade in the north and Navarrenx in the south. In addition, Soult called up the two divisions which were still in the Bayonne area. Beresford's Corps, on Hill's left to the north, was now on the move advancing towards Bidache. The weather at this stage became so bad, with sleet and snow, that the Allied advance was halted and those troops who were not in the front line were billeted in buildings. Wellington had achieved his aim of forcing the French eastwards. Now it was time to resolve the issue of Bayonne.

The Blockading of Bayonne – February 1814

Wellington's plan for Bayonne was straightforward. The River Adour was to be crossed between the town and the sea. When this had been achieved, Bayonne's lifeline would be cut and the blockade would be complete. Command of the operation was given to Sir John Hope who was to effect the blockade when the weather permitted. Wellington himself was preoccupied with the rest of his army in contact with Soult on the Gave d'Oloron. The method chosen for crossing the Adour consisted of hired boats sailing up the river to the appointed place and then being locked together to make a bridge. On the 22nd February the small flotilla of *chasse-marées* set sail from St Jean-de-Luz and headed for the Adour estuary. The 1st Division moved up to the river under cover, ready to cross the next day.

On the 23rd February, the 5th Division to the south of Bayonne threatened an attack in the hope of keeping the garrison's attention away from the river. However, because of a change in the wind, the flotilla of *chasse-marées* had been blown out to sea. Hope decided, nevertheless, to go ahead with the crossing rather than lose surprise. The crossing was made by ferrying men on pontoons and in small boats. It was a slow and hazardous business but fortunately it was generally unopposed. There was an approach by the French that

Bayonne from the Sand Hills.
From left to right: the Citadel, R. Adour, the town of Bayonne. Aquatint by Clark and Dubourg after Lt. G.B. Willis RA 1814

evening but not resolute and, after a few rockets had been fired at them, they withdrew.

By the next day, the 1st Division was on the north bank of the Adour and the brigades which were deployed in the sand hills were ready to defend the crossing should the French counter-attack. On the 24th the *chasse-marées* bridge was put into place again and, by the 26th, Hope's force had completed the river crossing. The next day the investment of Bayonne was accomplished with some 30,000 men who would remain committed to the blockade until the end of hostilities. Soult had now also left behind some 14,000 of his men in Bayonne and he effectively had to abandon the garrison to its own fate.

Lieutenant General Sir John Hope.
Engraved by J. Vendramini after W.M. Craig 1811

The Battle of Orthez – February 1814

While General Hope had been effecting the blockade of Bayonne with 1st and 5th Divisions, the remainder of Wellington's army had continued to press the French. Soult's line along the Gave d'Oloron was abandoned on the 24th February and the French withdrew in a north-easterly direction to the line of the Gave de Pau. Soult now concentrated his army in and around Orthez. He deployed four divisions on the high ground towards St Boès. Two divisions covered the ground down to Orthez and a third covered the river crossing in the town. Soult clearly felt that this was a tactically sound position from which to make a stand; high ground behind a river-line with good withdrawal routes. Although Soult only had some 36,000 men to Wellington's 44,000, the Orthez position was strong and to Soult's advantage.

Once Wellington realised that Soult intended to bring on a battle, he set about regrouping his forces to deal with the situation. Two divisions with cavalry were ordered to cross the Gave de Pau on the left near Peyrehorade and to move on the north bank towards Orthez. Further upstream, three more divisions with cavalry were to cross the river to the northern bank to make a combined five division force approaching Soult's right. At the same time, Hill's Corps was directed at Orthez town from the south.

The Allied attack against Soult's right in the area of St Boès started on the morning of the 27th February. Fighting was fierce and St Boès was taken but the French counter-attacked and the Allies were forced back. The French also started to push back Wellington's centre. Fortunately, the Commander-in-Chief himself saw a gap developing in the French defence and ordered a thrust to be made into the gap. This counter succeeded in separating the two main elements of Soult's force. Hill at Orthez had now crossed the river and was threatening Soult's left and rear. Soult decided to withdraw before his escape route northwards across the bridge at Sault-de-Navailles was blocked.

The Battle of Orthez.
Wellington being helped after his sword hilt was struck by a musket ball. Engraved by Reille after Martinet.

The French retreated across the Luy de Béarn at Sault, blew the bridge and headed north to Hagetmau and St Sever on the River Adour. Soult had been defeated but his army had not been destroyed. Casualties were relatively high with the French losing some 4000 men and the Allies some 2000. French morale was now low and during the retreat many French soldiers deserted. It was during the battle that Wellington's sword hilt was struck by a musket ball, driving it hard against his hip causing bruising and pain.

The Action at Aire-sur-l'Adour – March 1814

The French fell back on St Sever. Here Soult had to decide whether he moved towards Bordeaux to the north or towards Toulouse in the east. If he headed for Bordeaux he could entrap himself and at the same time leave southern France unprotected. Toulouse, on the other hand, was a fortified garrison where he could be resupplied and reinforced. He decided to head for Toulouse and, by pulling the Allies further inland, extend their lines of communications considerably. Although Napoleon had ordered Soult to take the offensive, he was not able to do so as his army was not in any fit state to take on the Allies again at this juncture.

Allied cavalry pushed ahead and as they approached St Sever, Soult pulled back eastwards to Grenade-sur-l'Adour. The Allied Light Division, consisting of the 95th Rifles and battalions of light infantry, was sent to capture the French depot at Mont-de-Marsan which had been abandoned by the French. By the 1st March, Wellington had established his Headquarters in St Sever. Allied divisions were moving east and Soult was pushed back to Aire-sur-l'Adour. From St Sever, Hill was dispatched south of the River Adour eastwards towards Aire. Under command, he had the 2nd Division, Le Cor's Portuguese Division, a brigade of British and King's German Legion dragoons, and a battery of horse artillery. He was tasked to locate the French. Similarly, the 3rd and 6th Divisions moved eastwards north of the river having crossed the Adour by fording it at St Sever.

The French were now withdrawing to Barcelonne-du-Gers and Soult had left a significant rear-guard at Aire to delay the Allied advance. Général Harispe's and Général Villatte's Divisions under Clauzel, were deployed immediately to the west of Aire-sur-l'Adour on high

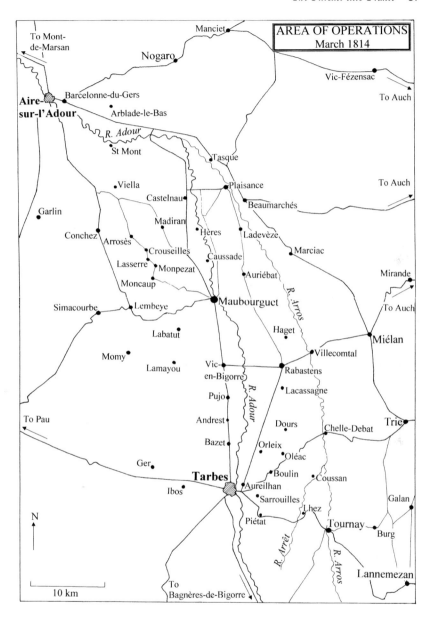

To Mont-
de-Marsan

Manciet

Nogaro

Vic-Fézensac

To Auch

Aire-
sur-l'Adour

Barcelonne-du-Gers

Arblade-le-Bas

R. Adour

St Mont

Tasque

To Auch

Viella

Plaisance

Castelnau

Beaumarchés

Garlin

Madiran

Hères

Ladevèze

Conchez

Arrosès

Crouseilles

Caussade

Marciac

Lasserre

Monpezat

Auriébat

Mirande

Moncaup

R. Arros

To Auch

Simacourbe

Lembeye

Maubourguct

Haget

Miélan

Labatut

Momy

Lamayou

Vic-
en-Bigorre

Rabastens

Villecomtal

R. Adour

Lacassagne

Pujo

To Pau

Andrest

Dours

Chelle-Debat

Trie

Bazet

Orleix

Ger

Oléac

Tarbes

Boulin

Coussan

Ibos

Aureilhan

Galan

Sarrouilles

Lhez

Piétat

Tournay

Burg

N

R. Arrêt

R. Arros

Lannemezan

10 km

To
Bagnères-de-Bigorre

AREA OF OPERATIONS
March 1814

ground, whilst D'Erlon's Corps remained north of the river. At about 2pm on 2nd March, Hill bumped Clauzel's rear-guard at Aire and decided to attack straightaway without forming the normal line of battle. Villatte's Division was quickly dislodged and retreated into Aire. Harispe's Division, however, provided stiff resistance and it was only when the attacking Portuguese were reinforced that Harispe withdrew. Soult quickly regrouped around Barcelonne and then moved south-eastwards on a broad front either side of the Adour towards Plaisance and Maubourguet. Wellington chose not to pursue the French and the two armies broke contact.

A fascinating insight is given of Hill's units as they moved forward to engage the two French divisions before Aire. Léonce, Baron de Claye recalled that one of his,

> *'childhood memories at St Jean (L'Abbaye Saint Jean de la Castelle near Duhort-Bachen) concerned the passage of the English in 1814 between the two battles of Orthez and Toulouse. We witnessed the spectacle of the combat at Aire where several hundred Spanish and Portuguese troops were out in the open because our courtyard and surrounding area were full of Scots and Hanovarians. I amused myself with them as they allowed me to mount their large horses but it horrified me to see them eat 'demi-couvés' goose eggs. They were the best people in the world and they were forced to be. The Provost Marshal took marauders and hanged them high and short for the least offence of theft. The officers paid ten times the value for essential provisions to such an extent that the locals, impoverished by a collapsing Empire, found themselves overflowing with guineas.'* [2]

Wellington paused at St Sever. Soult eventually had to be pursued but Bordeaux could not be ignored. It was a most important port and the French city authorities had indicated that they would declare for the King if given Allied support. Beresford was ordered to proceed to the city with 4th and 7th Divisions. Sir Rowland Hill wrote to his sister from Garlin, *'Soult's army is about four or five leagues from hence and our main force is halting while Marshal Beresford is marching two divisions to Bordeaux.'* [3] The 4th Division halted 35 kilometres short of the city at Langon to the south-east. Beresford and the 7th Division entered Bordeaux on the 12th March to a spontaneous welcome and completely unopposed. The city declared for the King and the inhabitants decorated their hats with the symbolic white cockade. Major Jenkinson, Royal Artillery, writing subsequently to Lieutenant Colonel Augustus Frazer stated that,

*'It is impossible to describe the joy and enthusiasm of the people at our entrance into this celebrated city …As soon as the usual salutations and compliments had passed, the Mayor drew from his pocket a paper, which he read in a most audible, dignified and manly voice. He came, he said, to express the joy and gratification of the inhabitants of Bordeaux at the approach of those who might be justly termed the saviours and deliverers of Europe; and to request the Marshal's [Beresford] permission to hoist the White flag and to declare for their legitimate sovereign, Louis XVIII, and at the very mention of which name the air was almost rent with cries of "Vive le Roi!", "Vivent les braves et les généraux Anglais!"' *[4]

With Bordeaux neutralized, Beresford, together with the 4th Division, was ordered on the 14th March to leave the 7th Division, under Lieutenant General George Ramsay, 9th Earl of Dalhousie, in the city and rejoin the main army. Wellington still had troops blockading Bayonne and needed to regroup what forces he could before giving chase once more to the French.

A Change in Direction Towards Tarbes – March 1814

At St Sever, Soult had concluded that his best option after the defeat at Orthez, was to head eastwards towards the safety of Toulouse and to abandon Bordeaux. As the Allies approached St Sever, the French retreated to Aire-sur-l'Adour and, when pushed out of Aire, turned south-eastwards towards Maubourguet and Tarbes. On the face of it, this seemed a strange direction. If Soult's intention was to head for Toulouse after Aire, he could easily have taken a due easterly route via Nogaro and Auch. This route, however, was exposed on both flanks and the French army, now known as *l'Armée des Pyrénées*, would have been extremely vulnerable in the relatively open countryside of the region. Instead, Soult chose a route where the lie of the land could offer him some protection. By heading south-east towards the mountains and then moving eastwards parallel to the Pyrenees, he would be less vulnerable. Also he might just be able to link up with Maréchal Louis Suchet's forces moving north out of Catalonia. In addition, by drawing Wellington south-eastwards, Soult effectively split the Allied army into two parts: the pursuing divisions and those left at Bayonne and Bordeaux.

During the first week of March, the French were well on their way south. As it happened, Soult received a letter from Général Henri

Jacques Guillaume Clarke, Comte de Hunebourg, Duc de Feltre, Napoleon's Minister of War giving the following directions:

Paris 7ᵗʰ March

The intention of the Emperor is that you pursue another direction immediately to your operations by making a flanking march which covers the Garonne and transfers the war to Pau via Tarbes so that you will always have your left against the Pyrenees.' [5]

The Emperor's instructions had been formulated before he knew that Soult was already heading towards Tarbes. Napoleon's aim in directing him to Pau clearly now could not be achieved. Soult had, however, developed a plan which was in the general spirit of the Emperor's wishes. By the 16ᵗʰ March, Soult was deployed on a line just north of Lembeye – Maubourguet. His Headquarters were at Simacourbe near Lembeye and his advance posts were out covering the whole line.

Wellington had now moved his Headquarters to Aire and had used the lull in the advance to reinforce. Three regiments from Morillo's Spanish Division had arrived from Navarrenx and the 4ᵗʰ Division from Bordeaux with Vivian's Hussar Brigade was to join the main body of the Army at any moment. The heavy cavalry of four brigades was also being regrouped with the main force after leaving their winter quarters in Spain. By the 17ᵗʰ March Wellington was ready once more to pursue the French. Since the engagement at Aire-sur-l'Adour on the 2ⁿᵈ March, there had been no significant contact between the two armies. A minor attempt on the 17ᵗʰ March was made by the French against the Allies' rear area at Hagetmau but was of no real consequence. Wellington grouped his forces into three columns. He deployed Hill as usual on the right with the 2ⁿᵈ Division and a Portuguese brigade, and Beresford on the left with the Light Division and Somerset's Hussars. As Sir John Hope, the third corps commander, was at Bayonne, Wellington commanded the centre column himself which consisted of a strong force including both 3ʳᵈ and 6ᵗʰ Divisions, and Bock's and Ponsonby's Heavy Cavalry Brigades, with Freyre's Spaniards following up. The general plan was to pursue Soult towards the Pyrenees and at the same time threaten his right and block his escape routes to Toulouse via Miélan and via Trie-sur-Baïse.

The Military Guinea of 1813.
Photograph courtesy of Spink and Son Ltd, London.

On the 17th March Maréchal Soult wrote to the Minister of War from his Headquarters at Simacourbe, *'that if the occasion presents itself to fall on one of their columns I will seize it with willingness [je la saisirai avec empressement].'* [6] Soult does, however, go on to say that, because of inferior numbers, he will not seek a major engagement.

'An Army Marches on its Stomach' (Attributed to Napoleon)

Both armies now had resupply problems. The French had lost their depots and magazines at both Mont-de-Marsan and at Aire-sur-l'Adour. Soult imposed severe requisitions on the local population and the French army generally just took what it needed, if it could be found. This policy was ruinous to local townspeople and farmers and inevitably supplies tended to be hidden.

The Allied army, on the other hand, was required by Wellington to pay for everything which was requisitioned even if exorbitant prices were being charged. In 1813, some 80,000 special gold guineas had been struck for Wellington's army as the French would only accept gold in payment for goods. This issue became known as the 'military guinea'.

Discipline was extraordinarily strict with floggings, deportations, and executions for relatively minor offences. This state of affairs contrasted with the French soldiery who were often ill-disciplined and whose behaviour was consistent with an army in retreat; tired, demoralized, and without proper subsistence. Sergeant William Lawrence of the 40th Regiment of Foot recounts:

> *'Lord Wellington had watched with hatred the many excesses committed by the enemy on the Portuguese and Spanish inhabitants during the late campaign and had determined to set for the future a better example; and accordingly he issued a proclamation that no plundering was to be carried on, on pain of death, which was to the credit of our noble commander.'* [7]

Captain Harry Ross-Lewin of the 32nd Regiment of Foot records that:

> *'On entering France, very strict orders had been issued to prevent plunder of any kind. A provost-marshal was appointed to every division, whose duty it was to ride round the bivouacs, to take up all stragglers found plundering and to punish them on the spot, should he think fit. His guard of cavalry were distinguished by white scarves, worn round the arm. The vigilance of the Provost Marshal had, of course, an excellent effect; but it is not in the power of man totally to put a stop to plundering in any army while stationed, during war in a foreign country.'* [8]

Wellington's policy in matters of the relationship between the Allied army and the local French population paid many dividends. It ensured that his army was well provisioned and that generally the Allies were seen more as deliverers and protectors rather than conquerors. The French army's unpopularity and poor reputation was also fuelled by the *levée en masse* conscription which had been organised in the region.

Ross-Lewin gives an interesting insight into another logistical problem. Such was the worn out state of many regiments' uniforms, they had to be sent back to the rear to reclothe and re-equip while at the same time escorting prisoners:

> *'My regiment marched with the Army until it arrived within twenty leagues of Toulouse, when it was ordered back to St Jean de Luz for new clothing. No-one who had ever before seen British troops could possibly have discovered at this period the original colour of our clothing; for it was so patched with a diversity of colours, and so bespoke a variety of wretchedness, that, with regard to this part of our equipment, we must have borne an undesirable resemblance to Falstaff's ragged regiment. We reached St Jean de Luz in eight days, and, having exchanged our tattered raiment for the new uniforms, set off again on the 18th March to rejoin the army.'* [9]

Although scrupulously fair in all his dealings, Wellington left no room for misunderstanding. For example, on the 15th March 1814, he issued Proclamation (No. 28) from Aire-sur-l'Adour to all the mayors of communes either occupied by Allied troops or through which the Allied Army would or might pass. In it the principles by which Allied requisitions were to be met were clearly defined. Local mayors and their deputies were to be held responsible for quickly and wholly executing all requisitions which were asked of them and this was to be done in liaison with Allied commissaries who were charged with the provisioning of the troops.[10]

The demands of the two armies totalling some 120,000 men and their horses, cutting a swathe through an under-populated countryside, were brutal. One division alone of 6000 men and 600 horses required each day 6000 loaves, 20 head of cattle, approximately 8 tons of straw or hay, 8 tons of cereals and many tons of wood.[11] Multiply these figures by a factor of 20 and the resultant figures give a rough idea of the daily consumption. It must also be borne in mind that Wellington's army and its host of camp followers advanced in the wake of the French who had already plundered the countryside by the time the Allies arrived.

The Eve of Action

The Allies Close on Tarbes

Now regrouped and reinforced, particularly with cavalry, Wellington issued the order for a general advance in three columns from the area of Aire-sur-l'Adour. The Allied army of some 50,000 men was once more on the move in pursuit of the French. On the right, Hill's Corps advanced south-east from Garlin via Conchez-de-Béarn. The centre column, with Wellington himself, moved via Castelnau and, on the left, Beresford's Corps moved on Plaisance. Wellington's Main Headquarters moved forward to Viella.

The Allied general advance was underway and unopposed. From Viella instructions were now issued for troop movement the next day. The full text of these instructions are as follows. Not only do they show clearly the plan but it is interesting to note the civility of the orders:

Viella, 18th March, 1814

The centre column will continue its march by the Vic-Bigorre road to Maubourguet, where it will receive further orders.

This column will be composed of the 3rd Division and Major-General Bock's brigade of cavalry, in the same order as this day, and the 6th Division, followed by Major-General Ponsonby's brigade of cavalry. This brigade of cavalry will move by Montus, Heres, and Caussade, if that *road is good; if otherwise, the brigade will join the column near Madiran, by the most convenient route.*

The pontoon train will follow the 6ᵗʰ Division until Major-General Ponsonby's brigade comes into the column, which brigade will then pass on in front of the pontoons.

The baggage of the troops above mentioned is to follow the troops in the order of the column.

Sir Thomas Picton will be so good as to put the head of the column in march at 7 a.m.

The Light Division and hussar brigade will move from Plaisance, by La Deveze to Auriebat, where the column will receive further orders.

The hussar brigade will communicate on the right with the column marching upon Maubourguet, by the great road from Aire to Vic Bigorre.

Lord Edward Somerset will be so good as to send a strong patrol from Plaisance to Marciac, and will communicate with that patrol from Auriebat.

The 4ᵗʰ Division will continue its march by the great road from Barcelonne to Plaisance.

The squadron of the 18ᵗʰ Hussars which is with the 4ᵗʰ Division will continue to move with it.

The Spanish corps will move to-morrow morning at daybreak by the villages of Rosès[Arrosès], Crouseilles, and Lasserre, to Moncaup, where it will receive further orders.

General Freyre will be so good as to move only two guns by the above route, and he will order the rest of the Portuguese artillery attached to the corps to get into the great road to Maubourguet, and close up to the rear of the 6ᵗʰ Division on that road. The baggage of head-quarters will move to–morrow to Maubourguet, there to receive further orders.' [12]

Soult's divisions were still on a line Lembeye – Maubourguet although, in the rear, units were now beginning to withdraw towards Tarbes. The French Commander-in-Chief was in no doubt about the danger he faced and recognised that his flanks were vulnerable. In another dispatch to Général Clarke, Minister of War, written at 4am on the 19ᵗʰ March from his headquarters at Momy, Soult recorded his version of events, *'the enemy was on the move and seemed to be looking for a way to outflank my side … the 13e Chasseurs which had been at Plaisance was forced to withdraw to Maubourguet.'* [13] He states there had been random firing from some of the outposts. That night Wellington's forces were seen establishing themselves on the high ground to the north-west of Maubourguet around Monpezat. Meanwhile, Soult redeployed his troops to the Labatut and Lamayou area west of Vic-en-Bigorre. Not only had he told Clarke in an earlier dispatch that he would fall on one of Wellington's columns *'avec empressement'* if given the chance, now in this most recent communication he bullishly states that *'it is highly likely that one of these days he* [Wellington] *will have a shock. I will be honoured to report the results.'*

Wellington's plan was that Beresford's Corps, consisting of Somerset's Hussars and the Light Division, should move fast on the left and cut the road Vic-en-Bigorre to Miélan thus eliminating one of Soult's escape routes. The other two columns would advance south towards Vic and Soult's main body. The three columns were to keep their line and maintain contact with each other.

The Combat at Vic-en-Bigorre

On the morning of the 19th March, Wellington's cavalry clashed with Soult's screen. Somerset's Hussars swept down on Rabastens and drove out the French flank-guard. At the same time, the dragoons of the King's German Legion under Von Bülow (Bock's Brigade) were involved in a skirmish north of Vic-en-Bigorre with Berton's Cavalry Brigade. Soult was seriously threatened and he now ordered Général Drouet, Comte d'Erlon to redeploy his two divisions to the area immediately north of Vic-en-Bigorre to block the Allied advance. D'Erlon, who had assumed command of the Centre Corps in July 1813, was an experienced officer having previously commanded at divisional level at Austerlitz. He deployed his 1st and 2nd Divisions to block Allied access to the main approach road to Tarbes. Général Berton's Cavalry Brigade, consisting of the 13e and 21e Chasseurs and the 2e Hussards, was then deployed on the French right in the vicinity of Rabastens to cover the access to Tarbes to the east of the Adour and to give some flank protection to D'Erlon's divisions. Meanwhile, Général Clauzel's Corps and Général Reille's Corps made their way south along small country lanes to the area near Ger, a small town to the west of Tarbes.

Lieutenant général Jean-Baptiste
Drouet, Comte d'Erlon.
Engraved by Antione Maurin.

D'Erlon's two divisions deployed just in time. Wellington and Lieutenant General Sir Thomas Picton, commanding 3rd Division, came forward protected by King's German Legion dragoons to assess the enemy's dispositions. Picton was ordered to attack supported by Major General Bock's Cavalry Brigade and by Lieutenant General Sir Henry Clinton's 6th Division. In General Picton's Memoirs it is recorded that:

'[The French] position was capable of a very obstinate defence … it was expected, from the nature of the ground, that the enemy would make considerable efforts to maintain this strong position; but the light companies of the division, supported by the Portuguese Brigade, met with little opposition, as they drove the French before them. The main body of the division moved close up in their rear, so that any attempt made in force by the enemy would have been immediately overcome; and the result was, that before evening, Sir Thomas Picton and his division encamped about 3 miles beyond the town of Vic Bigorre.' [14]

On Wellington's left the Light Division had moved from the area of Arblade-le-Bas on the 18th and, after crossing the River Arros at Tasque, had spent the night at Plaisance. Next morning it moved south to Auriébat, where it spent some hours during the afternoon, before continuing on to Haget, north of Rabastens. Captain Cooke of the 43rd Light Infantry in 1st Brigade of the Light Division records that:

'On the 19th having finished our march, we encamped on a ridge of hills, about five miles East of Vic-Bigorre which lay in a valley. About two o'clock P.M. we were ordered to stand to our arms, and on reaching the

summit of the hill, we saw the third division attack that town. The sun shone forth in full lustre, and a vehement fire of small arms and cannon almost enveloped with volumes of smoke, the scene of contest. We moved on the verge of the hills in a parallel line to turn the right flank of the enemy; – a heavy brigade of cavalry during the middle of the combat, turned the right of the French through the meadows close to Vic-Bigorre, and they were finally driven through the place. I hardly ever recollect a more delightful march than that we enjoyed towards the enemy. The sun was sinking behind the western hills, the surrounding country was wrapped in tranquillity, the din of war, had died away. The soldiers were tired, conversation ceased, and no sounds broke on the ear except the tread of the men's footsteps, or the planting of the horses' feet of the hussars, who were riding along in single files, or going off the side of the road, so as not to retard our march.' [15]

As D'Erlon's Corps was fighting its rear-guard action in the vineyards to the north of Vic-en-Bigorre, French artillery and baggage trains were also on the move south to Tarbes, many of the carts being pulled by oxen because of the shortage of horses. The sick and wounded were also making their way to the town. Soult had already moved his Headquarters from Momy to Tarbes and that night he lodged in the house of Comte Antoine Péré in the very centre of Tarbes. French delaying tactics had been relatively effective. As Soult had written earlier to Clarke, his intention was to avoid a general engagement. The rear-guard judiciously provided by D'Erlon's Corps had held up Wellington's advance long enough to allow the French to slip away to Tarbes. Casualties on the 19th March were light on both sides. Henry Sturgeon, an Assistant

Lieutenant général Comte Bertrand Clauzel.
Engraved by R. Young after Belliard.

Quartermaster General in the Royal Staff Corps, whom Wellington regarded as an officer '*of very superior merit*', was killed by a stray musket ball, in the head just under the eye, according to Judge Advocate Larpent, when riding recklessly forward during the 3rd Division engagement.

Soult had now lost the Vic to Miélan escape route east to Auch and on to Toulouse. In his dispatch from Tarbes, written at 4am on the 20th March, he praises Berton's cavalry, and the 21e Chasseurs in particular, for their action during the previous day. He goes on to state:

Lieutenant général
Comte Honoré Charles Reille.
Engraved by Francois Couché

'*Comte D'Erlon was able to repulse the English cavalry which had already entered the town [Vic-en-Bigorre] and he drove them back until 3p.m. Then several columns arrived simultaneously at Vic-Bigorre. The 1st Division was forced to retreat, it was well supported by the 2nd Division commanded by Général d'Armagnac and which was drawn up in parallel formation behind Vic-Bigorre. The engagement lasted into the night and Comte D'Erlon established his advanced posts at Pujo. He reported to me that there were many wounded.*' [16]

Soult had already made it clear to his commanders that if he were to make a stand now and fight Wellington, he would have to face a fully reinforced Allied army and he was in little doubt as to the outcome. He also realised that he would be cut off from Tarbes and that his escape to Toulouse would be blocked. Soult concluded that to take on the Allies now would court disaster and that it was more important that his army remain intact to fight another day. [17] The French withdrawal was orderly with little interference from the Allies. Reille's

Corps regrouped in the area of Ger to the west of Tarbes. Clauzel's Corps moved to Ibos also to the west of the town. D'Erlon remained near Pujo while Berton's cavalry brigade rested the night of the 19th just south of Rabastens.

Wellington, in his dispatch to Earl Bathurst, the Secretary for War, written on the 20th March, gives his account of the action at Vic-en-Bigorre:

Lieutenant General Sir Thomas Picton.
The London Printing and Publishing Co.

'[the enemy] on the 19th, held a strong rear guard in the vineyards in front of the town. Lieutenant General Sir Thomas Picton, with the 3rd Division and Major General Bock's brigade, made a very handsome movement upon his rear guard, and drove them through the vineyards and town.' [18]

En Garde!

The Allies came to rest on the night of the 19th March on the general line Vic to Rabastens. 4th Division with a squadron of 18th Hussars, returning from its deployment to Bordeaux, arrived back at Plaisance that evening, as did Vivian's Cavalry Brigade. Both formations would eventually join Beresford's Column on the left.

Maréchal Soult now found himself potentially in a very dangerous position. His army was deployed mainly to the west of Tarbes with a corps to the north. He was in no position to make a stand against Wellington and he must have known that the Allies were poised to pursue him on the morrow. The Pyrenees blocked the routes to the south so his only option was to evacuate Tarbes and its surroundings and head eastwards. The route Vic-en-Bigorre to Auch was now lost which left him only the Tarbes – Trie route and the Tarbes – Tournay route. Even so, to launch his army on either of these routes, he had to move his troops across the Adour via the small bridge at Tarbes.

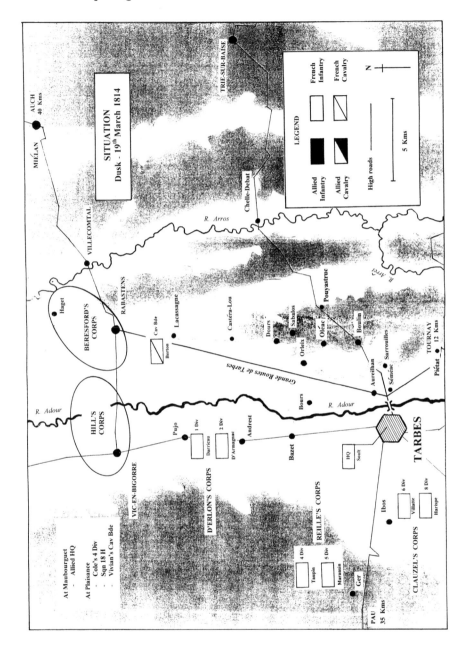

Of the two easterly escape routes open to Soult, the northern was vulnerable to attack and therefore, if he was able, Soult needed to protect this route for as long as possible. At this stage, therefore, the only safe route was the southern one via Tournay and Lannemezan. Soult and his generals had under command an exhausted army, on the defensive, and in retreat. The army was poorly equipped, lacking in horses, and many of the soldiers were without shoes. The local population was far from enamoured with it or its cause. The weather was foul, the tracks poor, the going difficult, and it was some 150 kilometres to Toulouse. The next few days were going to be testing. Soult, having made an assessment of his predicament, realized that he had to move his army quickly and that he needed to protect his

Lieutenant General Sir Henry Clinton.
Mezzotint by C. Turner after Sir Thomas Lawrence 1830.

vulnerable flank. At least moving close and parallel to the mountains was in the general spirit of his Emperor's original instructions.

By the evening of the 19th March, Wellington's main Headquarters was at Maubourguet and it was from here that the plans for the next day would be formulated and orders issued. Judge Advocate Larpent, who was at the Headquarters at Maubourguet, recalled in his journal that, '*Lord Wellington very late home.*'[19] Wellington could not know exactly how Soult would react to the predicament in which he found himself. Accordingly, the Allied plan needed to be sufficiently flexible to cater for any eventuality. He must have appreciated, however, that Soult, if threatened at Tarbes, would try and break clean in an easterly direction. Perhaps the Allies could cut off the French by taking a south-easterly route and by attacking their northern flank. The stage was set for what could be a momentous Sunday, the 20th March 1814. Both Commanders-in-Chief were about to have their generalship fully tested. Soult had an army to save and Wellington had a singular opportunity of defeating, if not destroying, the Army of the Pyrenees by turning its flank, blocking its escape and breaking it against the mountains. Wellington undoubtedly had the advantage but the canny Soult was not to be underestimated. It was not without good reason that Napoleon had once described Soult as '*Le Premier manoeuvrier d'Europe*'. Wellington similarly recognized him as an outstanding strategist although he was less generous in his comment on Soult as a tactician, '*he never seemed to know how to handle troops after the battle had begun*'.[20]

III

French Preparations and Allied Plans for the 20th March

The Movement of the French Army during the night of 19th March

During the night of Saturday 19th March 1814 the French army was not at rest and, before dawn on the 20th, all Soult's troops were on the move. D'Erlon's divisions which had formed the rear-guard overnight, withdrew from Pujo and Andrest, falling back to Tarbes where they again established a rear-guard in the streets and squares of the town. Meanwhile Reille's and Clauzel's Corps which had spent much of the night to the west of Tarbes started to move eastwards through the town and over the Adour. Clauzel's Corps was then to be deployed as the northern flank-guard and Reille's Corps would protect the subsequent withdrawal of D'Erlon's Corps through Tarbes and across the Adour. Soult had sent the convoys of field equipment, artillery, and wounded ahead to give them time to negotiate the steep climb up to Piétat just to the south-east of Tarbes on the Tournay road, so that they would not impede the withdrawing troops. Even so, it would take some time for the remainder of Soult's forces to pass across the narrow bridge over the river.

Soult had no illusions about the state of the army under his command which was desperately short of all supplies. Inevitably morale was very low, not only because of hunger and wretchedness but also because of disillusionment with the whole Imperial project in general and the war in Spain in particular. Soult knew that he was operating

Soult's Proclamation - 'Soldats!'
Issued on 8th March 1814 a few days after the French defeat at Orthez.
Courtesy of Les Archives Municipales de Tarbes.

in a region which, though French soil, was far from supportive. The local inhabitants, remote from Paris, were wearied by a decade of wars and they had watched as the French casualties were evacuated from Spain to the hospitals in their towns. They were still seeing their young men being conscripted to make up for these losses and put into front line regiments with minimal training. Now the Army of the Pyrenees was foraging and looting their farms and villages and it was little wonder that support for a Bourbon restoration was growing. Soult's fellow countrymen were sullen and resentful and only too ready to welcome the Allies. The mood was more anti-war than pro-Royalist. On the 8th March Soult had issued a powerful proclamation which he ordered to be printed in all local newspapers including that of Tarbes. It was a sweeping piece of propaganda against the 'perfidious English' and designed to warn the local inhabitants of the cost of defection and to strengthen the resolve of his soldiers. *'To Arms!'* proclaimed Soult, *'The cry resounds through the heart of the Empire! ...Soldiers! We condemn to the disgrace and general execration of all Frenchmen those who favour in any manner the insidious projects of the enemy. ...Honour and Loyalty, this is our motto. Fight to the last man the enemies of our august Emperor and our beloved France. ...Fight to the death those who try to divide us in order to destroy us and also those cowards who desert the Imperial Eagles to join another banner!'* [21]

Soult's plans for the 20th March

By now Soult had realised that any hope of attacking Wellington's advancing columns and destroying them piecemeal was gone. He was on the defensive and his priority was to retain the cohesion of his demoralised forces and redeploy them safely to Toulouse where significant supplies awaited them and they could recover behind the walls of the city and the protection of the River Garonne, at this time of the year swollen by Pyrenean meltwaters.

The protection of his northern flank as he executed a right-angled turn eastwards and the retention of two major routes from Tarbes to Toulouse were of utmost importance to Soult. He needed to extract his army from the Tarbes area while avoiding a flank attack and establish a new firm position by nightfall on the high ground some ten kilometres south-east of Tarbes on the Tournay road. The French deployment of their rear- and flank-guards therefore had to be completed by late morning as they headed eastwards. Soult would report the positions both on the high ground to the east of the Rabastens to Tarbes road and also in front of Tarbes on the road from Vic-en-Bigorre next day to the Ministre de la Guerre from Tournay,

> *The Army was deployed in position on the heights behind Tarbes, occupying the plateau of Oléac and was posted before Tarbes by 11am.* [22]

The French 1st Cavalry Division under the command of Maréchal Soult's brother, Général Pierre Soult, was to deploy astride the Tarbes – Trie road well out on the right flank. He planned to employ a screen of four cavalry regiments to watch the minor roads and tracks parallel to the Rabastens – Tarbes road and, in addition, to push the 13e Chasseurs further east watching the Villecomtal – Chelle-Debat road.

Maréchal Soult ordered the two divisions of Général Clauzel's Corps to occupy the high ground north of the Tarbes – Trie road. Général Eugène Casimir Villatte, a 44 year old veteran who had seen service in various armies including those of the Rhine and Italy, was to position his 6th Division on the Oléac – Boulin ridge. Clauzel also planned to place Général Jean Isidore Harispe's 8th Division on the high ground to the south of Orleix. Harispe, a 45 year old Basque, had been Suchet's chief-of-staff and had gained varied experience in Spain. He had commanded the 2nd Division in the East Coast Armies and when he was moved to under command Soult in early 1814 he took command of the reconstituted 8th Division. This deployment, coupled with that of 1st Cavalry Division, would create a significant force, which Soult hoped would keep the Trie road open, and would block or delay the Allies from turning his vulnerable right or northern flank.

In Tarbes itself, the French 4th Division, commanded by Général Taupin, another veteran of Austerlitz who joined Soult in 1813, was ordered to harass and delay the enemy to the west of the Adour bridge, supported by Maransin's 5th Division and Vial's Cavalry Brigade from a position on the rising ground across the river, east of Séméac. Then, after withdrawing over the river, Taupin was to create further delay from the hills to the east of Tarbes around Sarrouilles. He was also to send a mixed infantry and cavalry force augmented by artillery north to the village of Aureilhan, on the eastern outskirts of Tarbes, to provide a blocking force on the Rabastens road and the remainder of the Division would be deployed in the streets of Tarbes with a regiment and a squadron of cavalry kept centrally in reserve. This would allow D'Erlon's Corps to pull back through the town, cross the Adour, and head for the high ground east of Piétat where it could deploy again as a delaying force.

The Deployment of the Allied Army at dusk on 19th March

As Last Light fell on the 19th, Wellington's divisions were still moving up to the general line Vic-Bigorre – Rabastens. On the right, Hill's Column had joined the central group headed by 3rd Division which had moved forward to the southern edge of the town of Vic-Bigorre and just beyond. On the left, the Light Division had continued south from Auriébat along hills and ridges parallel to the

A rifleman of the 95th Rifles, a light dragoon, and a soldier of the 43rd Light Infantry. *From Goddard & Booth Military Costumes of Europe 1812.*

A Farm at Haget.
The Light Division bivouacked in and around the village on the night of 19ᵗʰ March.

River Adour which the soldiers could see to their right. An hour after Last Light, at about 7pm, the Division halted for the night at Haget in the hills 4 kilometres north of Rabastens and carried out its night routine to ensure its security. As the Allies were now in close contact with the French, outlying piquets of up to company strength per battalion were positioned forward and to the flanks by the brigade majors, the brigade commanders' chiefs-of-staff. It had now been some time since the Light Division had been engaged with the enemy but every man knew that tomorrow might well be testing. Although the sun had broken through the clouds during the afternoon, that night it was pitch black and overcast with rain threatening.

The 95ᵗʰ Rifles and the Light Division

An Experimental Corps of Riflemen had been raised by Colonel Coote Manningham in 1800 following the example of small bodies of sharpshooters and *Jägers* which had been formed in

American and German armies. The Corps was equipped with a rifle designed by Ebenezer Baker of Whitechapel who had submitted various proposals to the Ordnance Board. His first model, sent to the Experimental Corps on trial, was of the same length and calibre as the musket then in general service, with the intention of sharing a common ammunition with other infantry regiments and thus easing the Army's logistic problems. However, the officers of the Corps reported that both the rifle and standard load of rifle balls were too heavy for the riflemen to carry while conducting skirmishing tactics. Baker consequently submitted a shorter weapon of 45 inches with a bore of 0.625inches and twenty rifle balls to the pound. To compensate for the shortness of the rifle, compared with the musket, it was provided with a longer bayonet, known as a 'sword', for close quarter engagements. It was this model which was accepted by the Ordnance Board and went into production. The Corps's first engagement was in 1801 as sharpshooters in the rigging of Nelson's ships at the Battle of Copenhagen. In 1803 the Corps was renamed the 95th or Rifle Regiment and in subsequent actions, during the early phases of the war against France, it soon built up a firm basis of combat experience.

The men of the Light Division, bivouacked amongst the farms and hamlets around Haget, were veterans of the war in Spain and France. Formed at Shorncliffe by Major General John Moore in 1803 as the Light Brigade, in response to both the French invasion threat and developments in firearms technology, it consisted of the 43rd Light Infantry, the 52nd Light Infantry, and the 95th Rifles. The Brigade arrived in the Iberian peninsula in 1808 and played a major role in the retreat to Corunna during which Sir John Moore was killed. In 1810 the Brigade was increased to divisional size under Major General Robert Craufurd and fought in most of the major engagements in Spain. After Craufurd's death from wounds, suffered at the storming of Ciudad Rodrigo in 1812, the Division was commanded by a Hanoverian, Major General Charles, Baron von Alten, one of many German officers who had joined Wellington after the defeat of their forces by Napoleon at Jena in 1806. Appointed as a major general in the British Army in 1810, he initially commanded the German Brigade of 1st and 2nd Light Battalions King's German Legion until assuming command of the Light Division. Although not universally popular, Wellington thought well of him, calling him *'the best of Hanoverians'*.

The Rifles versus Muskets Controversy

There was considerable controversy in all European armies in the early nineteenth century over the arming of infantry units with rifles. No one doubted the rifle's greatly increased accuracy compared with the musket, which had an effective range of only 50 metres and had to be fired in mass volleys. Rifle equipped snipers, who could kill a man at 300 metres, had a part to play but for many commanders there were serious drawbacks to the wider use of rifles by infantry units. Rifles cost about three times that of a musket and were more complex to maintain. The major disadvantage was the longer time spent reloading as the tightly fitting balls often needed a small mallet to tamp them down the rifled barrel. At one round a minute the rate of fire was barely a third of that of musket armed units. It was for this reason that Napoleon had ordered the withdrawal of all rifles from service in his armies in 1807 in favour of the '1777 Year IX' musket. The 95th Rifles thus remained, if not still in name, an 'experimental' regiment, especially in the early years of the Peninsular War.

Throughout the War many commanders remained doubtful about the ability of rifle equipped units to operate without the close support of musket armed infantry. But these limitations had been demonstrably overcome by 1814. The Baker rifle, even in the heat of battle, could still easily outrange the musket and the rifle ball had a greater lethal or incapacitating effect. It was, however, the wider effect its introduction had for rifle troops which gave them their advantages. The technique of firing from cover, necessitated by the prolonged reloading, and changing firing position together with the

Musket and Rifle.
A British musket (top) and the shorter Baker Rifle with 'sword' bayonet.

Major General Charles, Baron von Alten.
Thomas Heaphy 1813. National Portrait Gallery.

loose formation of skirmishing led to an individual independence of action impossible in formed companies of musket armed infantry. Riflemen were encouraged to use initiative and develop an awareness and understanding of mutual support which gave rifle companies considerable flexibility of action. Such effectiveness as the 95th demonstrated was based not only on the original training at Shorncliffe but, crucially, on some six years of combat experience in the Peninsula. This experience provided the riflemen with the innate fieldcraft skills, much admired in the German *Jäger* regiments, which many had insisted were the prerequisite for rifle troops. The introduction of new weapons or weapon systems into armies always takes some time. Conservatism and prejudice must be overcome, troops have to be trained in new techniques and gain confidence, and the effect on tactics must be disseminated not only to other troops but,

Colonel Andrew Barnard.
Watercolour circa 1840 by an unknown artist

significantly, to senior commanders. Wellington understood the value of rifle troops well and employed them to good effect.

The Organization of the Light Division

In 1814, the Light Division consisted of the 1st Battalion 43rd Light Infantry, the 1st Battalion 52nd Light Infantry, and the 1st, 2nd, and 3rd Battalions 95th Rifles, formed into two brigades. It also included a Portuguese rifle armed battalion, the 3rd Battalion Caçadores. Normally the 95th battalions were allocated to the two brigades of the Division. They were never dispersed among the rest of the Army as was the 5th Battalion of the 60th Regiment, the only other British rifle armed regiment, whose companies were assigned to brigades to provide a screening force. From Salamanca onwards, the 95th remained concentrated in the Light Division and, at Vitoria, 13 of the available 19 rifle companies were allocated to Major General James Kempt's 1st Brigade of the Light Division. By 18th March 1814, for the first time, all three battalions of the 95th Rifles were concentrated in 2nd Brigade commanded by Colonel Andrew Barnard. In all, the total strength of the Brigade was about 1700 officers and men.

Andrew Barnard, himself a 95th officer, had originally commanded the 3rd Battalion, but after General Craufurd had been killed at Ciudad Rodrigo, he briefly took command of the Light Division during the storming of Badajoz. He subsequently reverted to the 1st Battalion and was severely wounded at the Nivelle when a musket ball pierced his right lung. Although he lost a quantity of blood, he made a swift recovery in time for Alten to appoint him to lead the 2nd Brigade. He was a much respected commander of rifle troops and one of his officers commented:

> *'He was one of the ablest of outpost generals. Few officers knew so well how to make the most of a small force. His courage, coupled with a thorough knowledge of the soldiers' character, was of that cool intrepid kind, that would at any time convert a routed rabble into an orderly, effective force. A better officer probably never led a brigade into the field.'* [23]

Light Division
(On 20th March 1814)
Maj Gen Charles, Baron von Alten

1st Brigade
Maj Gen James Kempt
1st Bn 43rd Light Infantry
1st Bn 52nd Light Infantry
3rd Bn Caçadores (Portuguese Lt Inf)

2nd Brigade
Col Andrew Barnard
1st Bn 95th Rifles
2nd Bn 95th Rifles
3rd Bn 95th Rifles

None of the participants at Tarbes seem to have recorded a reason why Alten, the divisional commander, had regrouped his three 95th battalions prior to 20th March, concentrating them in 2nd Brigade, although it was probably simply because Barnard had brought with him his own battalion on appointment to command the Brigade. He wrote to Lieutenant Colonel Alexander Cameron of the 95th Rifles in Holland, '*You will probably have heard that Lord Wn. has been so good as to move the 1st Bn. into the 2nd Brigade which gave me the command of it before commencement of the Campaign, the Battn. was on its way up from San Juan de Luz at the time of the Action at Orthes.*'[24]

Barnard's Brigade Major was Major Harry Smith, a veteran 95th officer. The 1st Battalion 95th Rifles was commanded by Lieutenant Colonel John Ross whose adjutant was Captain John Kincaid. Ross had two very experienced company commanders: Major Jonathan Leach and Lieutenant George Simmons. The 2nd Battalion was commanded by Lieutenant Colonel Amos Norcott and one of his company commanders was Captain John Duncan for whom the 20th March was to be a fateful day. Lieutenant Colonel Dugald Gilmour commanded the 3rd Battalion whose Quartermaster was a William Surtees. It was these officers and others in the Light Division whose eyewitness accounts have been used extensively in this narrative. Captain William Cox, Lieutenant James Gairdner, and Sergeant Costello were all of the 95th Rifles and their accounts have also been invaluable. Captain Cooke of the 43rd and Major Blakiston, commanding the Light Division's Caçadores battalion, recorded the events as they saw them unfold. All these individuals were experienced Light Division soldiers and were thus able to record the events both accurately and realistically from their perspective.

Wellington's Plan

Wellington saw a possible opportunity at Tarbes to deliver a *coup de grâce* to Soult's army by pinning it against the Pyrenees mountains and if not destroying it, then containing it in the foothills and narrow valleys until the war in the north and political events had played out to a satisfactory conclusion. To achieve this he would have to sever all Soult's escape routes eastward towards Toulouse which he correctly surmised was Soult's next goal. Wellington had already denied the use of the northern of Soult's three possible routes east, the road from Rabastens via Miélan and Mirande to Auch. In order to cut the remaining two routes, he would have to move early in the morning, transfer significant forces to his left column and outflank or drive in any French right flank defences. With this in mind, he decided that the 6th Division and the Spanish Corps, together with a considerable cavalry force, would join the left column. Beresford would thus command a powerful force with the intention of closing the Tarbes trap.

Wellington's plan for the 20th March was to advance in two main columns towards Tarbes, one either side of the River Adour. Hill was to advance on the right along the Vic-en-Bigorre road to Tarbes with Stewart's 2nd Division, Picton's 3rd Division, Le Cor's Portuguese Division, and Morillo's Spanish Brigade. Hill's column also included a strong cavalry force of Fane's Light, and Bock's and Clifton's Heavy Brigades. On the left, Beresford's Corps consisted of Clinton's 6th Division, Alten's Light Division, Freyre's Spanish Corps, and, under General Sir Stapleton Cotton, Somerset's Light Cavalry and Ponsonby's Heavy Cavalry Brigades. Meanwhile the 4th Division and Vivian's Hussar Brigade had only just arrived from Bordeaux, reaching Plaisance on the 19th March after a long and tiring march on bad roads and in foul weather. They still had to catch up with the main force

Orders to the Allied Army for the 20th March

On the evening of 19th March, the following Operation Order was issued from Wellington's Headquarters at Maubourguet.

'ARRANGEMENT FOR THE MOVEMENT OF THE ARMY ON THE 20TH MARCH.

Maubourguet, 19th March 1814

The Army will move forward to-morrow in two columns upon Tarbes.

The right column will be composed of the 3rd Division and Major-General Bock's brigade of cavalry, and the troops under the immediate orders of Lieutenant-General Sir Rowland Hill. This column will move by the direct road from Vic Bigorre to Tarbes. It will be prepared to march from Vic Bigorre at 7½ a.m.; but Sir Rowland Hill will not put the column in motion till directed to do so. Sir Rowland Hill will allot such force as he may think expedient to move through the country on the right flank of the column and cover its march on that side.

The left column of the army is to assemble at Rabastens; and it will be directed from thence upon Tarbes, by the great road leading from Rabastens to that place. This column is to be composed of the Light Division and hussar brigade, followed by the 6ᵗʰ Division and Major-General Ponsonby's brigade of cavalry. All these troops will move so as to be before daybreak at Rabastens, and will form the column in the order above mentioned. The column is not to move on, however, from Rabastens till ordered to do so.

The Spanish division under General Freyre will also belong to the left column, and will close up to the other troops above mentioned.

The 4ᵗʰ Division is to move tomorrow morning, at as early an hour as possible, upon Rabastens, and Sir Lowry Cole will be so good as to send forward to that place a report of his progress.

The baggage of the troops composing each column of the army is to move in rear of the column in the same order as the troops.' [25]

It is of interest that no mention of 2ⁿᵈ Division is made in orders during this phase of the campaign. The Division is included in an order on 1ˢᵗ March and in a report by Hill of 3ʳᵈ March. There is no further mention of 2ⁿᵈ Division again until the Battle of Toulouse but there is no evidence that the Division had been detached on some special task. In a close study of the General and Specific Orders it becomes clear that Hill, a trusted and experienced corps commander whom Wellington allowed considerable freedom of action, had 2nd Division permanently under command. Other infantry, cavalry, and Iberian divisions and brigades were occasionally removed or returned but 2ⁿᵈ Division stayed with Hill. Moreover, Hill was often, if not always, advancing on his own separate axis. Wellington was constantly switching the other corps about and orders needed to keep specifying regroupings and, where troops were under direct command of the C-in-C, axes and objectives. With Hill none of this detail was necessary; he was given his orders which consistently repeat the phrase "the troops under the immediate orders of". It therefore seems reasonable to infer that 2ⁿᵈ Division and some other infantry and cavalry regiments were permanently under Hill's command during this period. Interestingly, Lieutenant General Sir William Stewart, the commander of 2ⁿᵈ Division, had, as a lieutenant colonel in 1800, trained the Experimental Corps of Riflemen in shooting and tactics.

On the face of it, Wellington's plan was not unreasonable. He had clearly appreciated Soult's predicament. He had realised that escape to the east was Soult's only option other than to fight it out in and around Tarbes itself. What Wellington seems to have failed to appreciate was the extent to which, during the night of the 19th and the early hours of the 20th, Soult would be able to redeploy his divisions and thus create a more advantageous position for himself. As the 20th of March dawned, the Allied army was still on a line Vic-en-Bigorre – Rabastens whilst the French were already on the move east. Overnight, Soult had cleverly created a tactical advantage and had put himself in a good position to execute a difficult withdrawal in an orderly fashion.

IV

Sunday the 20th March –
The Allies Engage the French

Early Morning on the 20th March

Most of the soldiers in the Allied army had not reached their bivouac areas until at least an hour after dusk and they then had to make do with a hurried meal around small camp fires. There were few hours of sleep as the whole army had to be up and preparing to move in order to be at the start point for the day's advance before dawn.

In the farms and hamlets around the village of Haget, the Light Division was up particularly early. Just after 3am Harry Smith, the Brigade Major of 2nd Brigade, ordered his bugler to sound the first preparatory call which was echoed by the battalion commanders' buglers. The sergeants ensured that the men were up and dragging on their packs and equipment. The baggage was packed and finally loaded on to the horses and mules of the baggage trains while junior officers checked that their companies were ready to move. At 4.15am the buglers sounded 'Rouse' calling companies to form up while all the night guards and inlying piquets rejoined their companies. Meanwhile, the regimental baggage was assembled under the orders of the quartermasters ready to be centralised as specified by the Division's Adjutant & Quartermaster General. Fifteen minutes later buglers ordered the 'Advance' and, preceded by the outlying piquets, which had been providing security overnight, the Division marched through the darkness by tracks and lanes along the small ridges which led down to Rabastens. Here it joined the 6th Division, which was already assembled and prepared to move. The Light Division took

The High Road from Vic-en-Bigorre to Tarbes.
Little has changed since 1814 and now the D935 along which Hill's Column advanced on Tarbes.

up its normal position at the head of the Column with a screening force of 10th Hussars from Somerset's Light Brigade. This arrangement allowed the faster moving light infantry to deploy rapidly should the Column suddenly be engaged by the enemy.

On the right flank, Hill had sent forward his cavalry screen to observe the movement of the French rear-guard, as it withdrew from Pujo, while the remainder of his force was poised at the southern outskirts of Vic-en-Bigorre by 7.30am. On receipt of orders, brought by an ADC who had galloped over from Wellington's forward Headquarters, Hill ordered his Column to advance south on the high road to Tarbes.

Meanwhile on the left flank, the Light Division, leading Beresford's Column, had also been ordered to advance. 2nd Brigade passed through Rabastens which had been held overnight by Somerset's cavalry. James Gairdner thought Rabastens *'a very good looking town'*. 1st Brigade skirted the town to the west and the Division then advanced in column down the tree-lined *'Grand Route de Tarbes'* which ran straight and true flanked by hedges and dikes.

The Adour Valley and the hills round Tarbes

The River Adour rises in the Pyrenees and after passing Tarbes on its eastern edge flows north through a broad alluvial valley covered with fertile farmland. At this time of year the Adour was swollen by melting snow from the mountains. The road from Vic-en-Bigorre to Tarbes, the route Hill's Column would follow, runs south along the valley with the river on its east side. To the west of the road a range of low hills lies about 4 kilometres away and the country is generally open with only two small villages on the road south of Pujo. On the eastern side of the Adour, the road from Rabastens to Tarbes also keeps to the valley floor but the country to the east of this road is broken by a succession of ridges some 100 metres in height above the valley floor and reaching out northwards from the foothills of the Pyrenees. About 4 kilometres after leaving Rabastens, the first low ridge appears 500 metres from the road at the village of Lacassagne and after a similar interval another ridge leads up to the village of Dours. This ridge continues rising gently through the villages of Sabalos and Oléac where there is a tower at its highest point. After a further 4 kilometres along the main road, a third undulating ridge begins just beyond Orleix which overlooks the main road. At

The 'Grande Route de Tarbes'
The high road to Tarbes from Rabastens along which Beresford's Column advanced on Tarbes. Engraved by Jacques Couchés after Christophe Civeton.

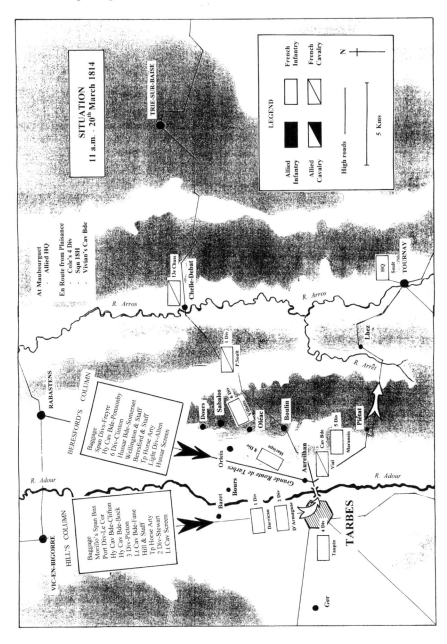

OLÉAC
TELEGRAPH TOWER

OLÉAC

The Oléac Ridge.
Looking east from the Rabastens – Tarbes road near Orleix. Note the telegraph tower on the crest.

its southern end, this ridge joins the hill around Piétat and dominates the south-eastern exits from Tarbes. A deep fast running stream, the Canal d'Alaric, runs along the western foot of this ridge supplying water to the villages and power for the watermills. Between the Oléac and Orleix ridges is a flat-bottomed valley one kilometre in width which leads south to the Tarbes – Trie road at Boulin and on to the village of Sarrouilles. The steep slopes of these ridges were covered in thick brushwood in 1814 but the crests of the ridges and the valley floors were cultivated with vines, trained high in the local manner, and other crops, including cereals, fruit and chestnut plantations. This was not good cavalry country but was most suitable for infantry operations, especially skirmishing.

The Allied Advance

On the right, Hill's Column advanced southwards across the open country of the Adour valley through the village of Pujo, recently evacuated by D'Erlon's rear-guard, and on to Andrest with no serious contact with the enemy. The 2nd Division led behind a screen of light dragoons and was followed by Fane's Light Cavalry Brigade. Next came the 3rd Division, Bock's Heavy Cavalry Brigade, Le Cor's Portuguese Division, and Morillo's Spaniards, followed by Clifton's Heavy Cavalry Brigade.

On the left, the Light Division advanced with a cavalry screen provided by the 10th Hussars followed by 2nd Brigade, then 1st Brigade, with E Troop Royal Horse Artillery, commanded by Lieutenant

Richard Hardinge, bringing up the rear. Beresford and his aides and then Wellington and his staff rode close behind, followed by the remainder of Somerset's Hussar Brigade. Next came General Clinton's 6th Division searching for a route up onto the wooded ridges in an attempt to outflank the French right. Freyre's Spanish Corps followed on and behind stretched the baggage train. Cole's 4th Division, with Vivian's Hussars, was still many kilometres behind but marching hard in order to catch up.

At the head of Beresford's Column, the high road allowed the Light Division to proceed at a good pace, marching briskly at four kilometres in the hour with three men abreast. Company commanders rode at the rear of their companies while the battalion commanders moved up and down the lines of their men. There was little chatter among the ranks as 'Black Bob' Craufurd, of immortal memory, had always insisted on silence on the march. The Division's column stretched some 2 kilometres along the road and 6th Division waited in Rabastens until after 8.30am when the road became clear for it to move forward. The leading 10th Hussars squadron protected the advance by deploying vedettes, each a troop of hussars, out on the flanks especially on the left where small hamlets and the edges of the wooded ridges could provide cover for French light troops or *voltigeurs*. Some 8 kilometres from Rabastens the 6th Division, supported by the 15th Hussars of Somerset's Cavalry Brigade, was ordered to begin its wide sweep to the east in an attempt to turn the French right flank. Near the village of Castéra-Lou, 6th Division left the main road at about 10am and moved up along the ridge which led to the

POINT 333   POINT 348

The Orleix Ridge.
Looking east from the Rabastens – Tarbes road just south of Orleix. It was from here that Somerset's Hussars first spotted the French Voltigeurs. The lake is modern.

village of Dours, but made no contact with the enemy at that stage. Meanwhile Hill, on the right, was advancing steadily against D'Erlon's troops who were retreating down the main road before him and by 11 o'clock the leading troops of Hill's Column had reached the area of Bazet.

The French Right Flank Deployment

As the Allies advanced south towards Tarbes, Soult's divisions had been moving to their assigned positions and were in place by 11am. Clauzel's divisions were ordered to secure the Tarbes – Trie road by occupying the ridges north of the road. Général Villatte's 6th Division was stationed on the Oléac-Boulin ridge while Général Harispe's 8th Division, some 4,500 strong, was positioned to the left

French Infantry of the Line – 1808.
On the left a Grenadier, on the right a Voltigeur. Engraved by R. Bellarge.

Général de Division Comte Jean Isadore Harispe.
Lithograph Lamaignere à Bayonne. Courtesy of Musée Basque et de l'histoire de Bayonne.

of 6th Division on the ridge south of Orleix, which looks down on and dominates the Rabastens – Tarbes road. Harispe deployed Général de Brigade Guilhem Dauture's Brigade of some 2,000 men, with its three light infantry *léger* battalions, forward to dominate the main Rabastens road. Harispe retained Général de Brigade Jean-Baptiste Baurot's Brigade on the summit of the ridge. This brigade, of some 2,500 men, was a powerful but unwieldy force of six line regiments, although 117e de Ligne was barely up to two company strength. Baurot placed his regiments straddling the crest where some existing ditches and dikes formed natural defence works, allowing them to maximise their firepower. 45e and 116e de Ligne were deployed in the centre, while at least two regiments were retained in reserve. Neither of the French 6th nor 8th Divisions were allocated any artillery as Soult did not intend to fight a pitched battle on this flank. Meanwhile Reille ordered Général Taupin's 4th Division to delay the Allied advance through Tarbes. He pushed an infantry regiment augmented by cavalry and two artillery pieces up the Rabastens road beyond the edge of the village of Aureilhan. Soult rode up onto the crest of the ridge by Harispe's 8th Division and saw through his

95th Riflemen in Action.
Showing different firing positions with the Baker Rifle. Etched by Rowlandson.

telescope the leading regiments of all the columns and estimated in a subsequent report that there were '*about six thousand cavalrymen*' advancing towards his various positions.

The Forces Engage

The Light Division continued its advance without incident until the head of the column had passed the village of Orleix on its left and was within about 3 kilometres of Tarbes, when the leading hussars spotted a body of French *voltigeurs* in the edge of a wood south of the village. Captain Cooke of the 43rd Light Infantry noted:

> '*Within a short distance of Tarbes the hussars rode forward, and pushed their line of vedettes half way up the hills to the left of the road, with their carbines resting on their thighs, and within one hundred yards of the French infantry, who did not fire, although stationed on the verge of the wood.*' [26]

The 2nd Brigade quickly closed up behind the cavalry and it became clear that the hussars had identified the forward edge of a sizeable

French position. Meanwhile Kincaid also saw *'what appeared to be small piquet of the enemy, on the top of a hill to our left, looking down upon us, when a company of our second battalion was immediately sent to dislodge them'* [27] and Wellington rode forward to get a good view of the enemy positions. With his usual coolness he *'took a peep at the enemy's position (our columns were at the same time concentrating) with the eye of an eagle, and ordered the different columns to advance to their different points'*, noted Simmons. [28] Wellington conveyed his orders directly to Colonel Barnard, the Brigade Commander, bypassing Alten, the Divisional Commander, who was not unused to being treated in this manner. It was now approximately 11.30am. Initially a company of the 2nd Battalion 95th was sent to dislodge the *voltigeurs* from the edge of the wood a few hundred metres to the east of the road but as they attempted to do so it became apparent that the French were in much greater strength than first appeared. Soon the whole of the 2nd Battalion and the left wing of the 1st under Major Jonathan Leach were committed. As the rifle companies doubled forward the 10th Hussars gave them an *'encouraging huzza'* and the 3rd Battalion moved up in support. John Blakiston, whose Portuguese 3rd Caçadores were in 1st Brigade, watched the advance from the road and thought, *'Nothing could exceed the manner in which the 95th set about the business.'* [29]

As the rifle battalions of 2nd Brigade deployed east, off the main Rabastens-Tarbes road towards the woods to their left, 1st Brigade closed up behind the hussar screen which was now faced by several troops of *chasseurs à cheval* astride the road who tempted the hussars to charge. They declined and a battalion of 1st Brigade, the 43rd Light Infantry, attempted to creep along the hedgerow bordering the road in order to ambush the French cavalry but were then unfortunately discovered. The *chasseurs* repeatedly attempted to draw the hussars forward and then suddenly wheeled about revealing the two light artillery pieces which instantly fired at 'half-range' but both balls flew low over the hussars' heads.

Meanwhile, on the right, Hill's Corps reached Tarbes without too much difficulty. Blakiston continues, *'Shortly afterwards a smart firing began to the westward of the town, which we found to proceed from Sir Rowland Hill; he was engaged with the enemy who occupied a position in that direction.'* [30]

Cautiously, Stewart's and Picton's Divisions started to move into and through the town followed by the Portuguese Division and Morillo's Spaniards. They met with token opposition and delaying tactics from Taupin's Division which, at this juncture, had a regiment supported by a squadron of cavalry in the Grande Place de Tarbes. The Allies met a large crowd of citizens, largely made up of women, who greeted the soldiers with shouts of *"Vive l'Angleterre! Vive les Bourbons!"*[31] Other elements of Taupin's and Maransin's Divisions were already across the Adour in supporting positions on the high ground east of Tarbes on the road to Tournay.[32]

The Attack by 2ⁿᵈ Brigade

The brushwood and trees on the steep slopes of the Orleix ridge provided good cover for Dauture's three *léger* battalions which had been deployed forward of the main force of Harispe's 8th Division as a screen. After crossing some damp meadows the rifle companies of the 2ⁿᵈ Battalion 95th Rifles encountered the tree-fringed Canal d'Alaric and waded across, waist deep. Simmons recorded, *'There was a small river in front of the position, the hills occasionally patched with clumps of brushwood and trees, which assisted the enemy much, as he had the opportunity of hiding his columns.'* [33] The French *voltigeurs* of the *léger* regiments were moving back into the woods and up the steep slope engaging the 95th when they could. Once established on the edge of the wood, the riflemen began skirmishing their way up the wooded hill under intense fire and suffered several casualties. By this time it became clear that they faced more than a light screen of French sharpshooters and that the enemy was in considerable strength. The remainder of the 1st Battalion was deployed to the left and the 3rd Battalion moved up on the 2ⁿᵈ Battalion's right flank. The whole of

Canal d'Alaric.
Simmons recorded that 'there was a small river in front of the position'.

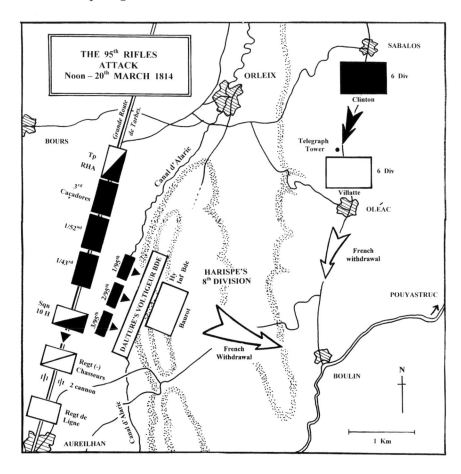

2nd Brigade was now committed to the attack, forming a continuous skirmishing line as the riflemen struggled up the steep slope through the dense brushwood, taking up firing positions behind trees and only pausing to reload and catch their breath. Higher up the slope the voltigeurs *'occupied the hedges and dikes on the high ground, from which it was necessary we should dislodge them.'* [34] recalled Surtees. Eventually they emerged at the summit and confronted Baurot's heavy regiments. Sergeant Costello, mistaking the natural banks and dips for defensive earthworks, recorded:

'The French had thrown up strong entrenchments, and were, to use a nautical phrase, 'tier above tier'. I never remember to have been so warmly engaged as on this occasion, except at Badajoz. The enemy were in great numbers, our attacking force few, being only our three battalions of Rifles which their bullets were fast thinning as we struggled up the hill.' [35]

There followed an intense firefight at close range in which the 3rd Battalion found itself in closest contact with the French line infantry on the crest of the ridge. It was a bitterly contested engagement with the riflemen in their skirmishing lines, using what cover they could find, closing in towards the centre of the French position where the men of the line regiments stood firing in three ranks. The 95th suffered many casualties: Captain Duncan of the 2nd Battalion was killed, Lieutenant Colonel Norcott, riding along the line on his black mare, was severely wounded in the shoulder and Major George Miller had to assume command of the 2nd Battalion. In addition many other officers, sergeants, and riflemen were hit. But there were lighter moments as when a captain was knocked down by a French musket ball and carried to the rear by his men. However, he suddenly revived and called out *"Stop, let me feel!"* and finding that he had been struck on his drinking flask and was unharmed, leapt out of their arms and headed back to his company where he was greeted with shouts of laughter.[36]

Général Harispe was determined to maintain his blocking position on the ridge and ordered Baurot's reserve battalions to carry out a right flanking counter-attack against the 95th's line. It has been conjectured that Harispe, seeing the riflemen's green uniforms thought them to be Portuguese troops and thus more easily repulsed.[37] John Blakiston observing the action from the road recorded:

Général de Division Eugène Villatte, Comte d'Outremont.
Courtesy of Collection of Alain Pigeard.

'When they [our Rifles] had nearly gained the top of the hill, the French, thinking to surprise them, sent a strong party round the side of the hill to take them in the flank. We, who being a greater distance, saw the manoeuvre, trembled for our poor fellows, who could not be aware of the attack. Luckily, however, one of the riflemen, who was on a flank, caught sight of the column, and gave the alarm, when instantly the nearest men collected the number of about sixty, fixed their swords on their rifles, and just as the enemy appeared round the brow of the hill, charged them though at least twice their own number, and sent them back faster than they came.'[38]

In all, Baurot launched three counter-attacks with his reserve battalions but all were repulsed by the 95th's 1st Battalion which took the brunt of the attacks. On the main position, the greater accuracy and range of the Baker rifle was beginning to take its toll on the lines of French infantrymen firing musket volleys. In 116e de Ligne, a company commander, Capitaine Tolly, was killed, two lieutenants wounded, and fifty or more NCOs and privates hit. In 45e de Ligne, Lieutenant Sainte-Marie was killed, Capitaine Guillin wounded, and a considerable number of further casualties incurred. Eventually Harispe, realising that he could not keep his Division under such

Général de Brigade
Jean-Baptiste Baurot.
Courtesy of Collection of Alain Pigeard.

withering fire for much longer and aware that Villatte to his right was under attack from Clinton's 6th Division and likely to fall back at any moment, ordered a withdrawal. His Division had put up a stiff resistance and William Cox admitted that Harispe's men had *'fought remarkably well here'.*[39]

As the rifle companies advanced through the abandoned position they were amazed at the toll their rifle fire had inflicted on their opponents. The vineyards near the scene of action were covered with the killed and wounded. Sergeant Costello had some regrets,

> *'I was very sorry this day for striking a poor Frenchman whom I came up with, as I discovered he was badly wounded; but I made an amende honorable by a sup from my canteen, which he received with grace.'*[40]

Harry Smith, the Brigade Major, recalled:

> *The loss of the enemy from the fire of the Rifles was so great that one could not believe one's eyes. I certainly had never seen the dead lie so thick, nor ever did, except subsequently at Waterloo. Barnard even asked the Duke to ride over the hill and see the sight, which he consented to do, saying, "Well,*

Barnard, to please you, I will go, but I require no novel proof of the destructive power of your Rifles." '[41]

Colonel Barnard writing a few days later, summed up the whole action:

'*The 2nd Batt. was sent on a ridge to the left of the road from Rabastens to Tarbes to observe a corps of French who occupied the further end of it having their advance posted in a small wood which was strong from its situation and the form of the ground. I was desired to send some skirmishers to drive them out and three companies of 1st Batt. under Leach walked them out in a few minutes – Lord Welln. had ordered in the meantime the whole division up to the point where 2nd Batt. were. The 2nd Batt. advanced to the support of Leach as soon as he gained the wood and protected his right, the enemy formed a considerable body of men and made a very spirited attack on the companies which occupied the wood and had turned their left when Gilmour brought up the other three companies of the 3rd Batt. to that point and put them to an ignominious flight in a moment. The 3rd Batt. in the meantime had attacked up the hill in front of our right and driven the enemy from that point – I assure you the rifles were laid very strait the enemy lost as many men as I think it possible to be knocked over in so short a time – the beauty of the business was that we were formed and ready for another attack in a few minutes, Lord W. saw the whole and was most pleased with the rapidity with which the Corps made its attacks and equally so with the quickness with which they got together when it was over.*'[42]

TARBES   POINT 348

The Orleix Ridge from Oléac.
Looking west from Oléac. In the middle distance the Orleix ridge rises to Point 348 in the centre.

Meanwhile, General Clinton's 6th Division, having approached the village of Oléac through Sabalos along the ridge from Dours, could be seen attacking Villatte's Division formed round the tower near Oléac, which the British referred to as a windmill, by an extended cannonade and a brief skirmish. Lieutenant John Malcolm of the 42nd Regiment described the scene, *'We had just arrived upon the scene of action, and had begun to hear the spent balls flying past, when the enemy gave way. The action, however, still continued upon our right* [the 95th Rifles attack against Harispe's Division]*; but by a movement made by General Clinton with the sixth division, by which their rear was threatened, they gave way in all directions.'* [43] This action was observed by staff officers and curious local inhabitants from the village of Bours, some 4 kilometres to the west in the Adour valley; *'The battle as it unfolded along the ridge at Oléac, was watched by red-coated officers of the English Army from the bell tower of Bours church.'* [44] Likewise, Lieutenant John Meyricke of the 43rd Light Infantry, in the uncommitted 1st Brigade of the Light Division, wrote to his father, *'I never had so good a view of any affair, the Army moved on in four Columns, the Heads of each in a line, both armies manoeuvred beautifully … his* [Soult's] *men fought well as a number of them were knocked over.'* [45]

Buttons and Balls.
Buttons of 25e Léger (Harispe's Div.), 43e de Ligne (Taupin's Div.), 95th Rifles (a modern copy), 103e de Ligne (Villatte's Div.). From the left: Two British musket balls (19.5mm), two Baker rifle balls (16mm), and two French musket balls (17mm).

A battery of Allied horse artillery in support of Hill's Corps meanwhile had set itself up just to the north of Tarbes on the west bank of the Adour and was able to harass Taupin's troops. Those elements of Taupin's Division still in Tarbes and on the west of the bridge now started to withdraw to the right bank of the river. This withdrawal was covered by the 12e Léger of Taupin's Division which was deployed to the north and south of the road in the vines and amongst the numerous hedges which criss-crossed the terrain. It was not until about 2 o'clock that Hill's troops managed to cross over the river and onto the east bank. It is difficult to understand why the French failed to destroy this key bridge over the Adour at Tarbes although there is evidence that it was barricaded and defended by a group of patriotic citizens. This classic failure allowed Hill's troops to spill out from Tarbes in pursuit at the very time the French were trying to make their escape and to delay the Allies. However, the country to the east of the river was intersected by a series of narrow but deep

Bours Church.
'The battle ... was watched by red-coated officers of the English Army from the bell tower ...' Gibaud

streams and the pursuing squadrons of Fane's Light Dragoons were forced again and again to return to the high road. As a result, Taupin's rear-guard managed to break contact and climb up the hill to Piétat. The parish priest, Father Bertres, described the events in a letter to the Comtesse de Chateaurenard,

> *'Sunday the 20th in the morning, our army gained the heights of Sarrouilles which dominated the town of Tarbes and the superb plain of Bigorre. All day we heard the cannons and muskets as though we were on the battlefield. At 2pm it seemed to us that the army withdrew towards Tournay.'* [46]

Hill now established himself to the east of Tarbes but continued to be held up by French artillery which had been sited on the high ground to the east of the town. Taupin's Division and other withdrawing French troops did not linger in the area as they risked being cut off by some of Beresford's troops who were threatening their northern flank from the Oléac – Boulin direction.

Tilting at the 'Windmill'

Historians have placed the centre of the 95th Rifles action around a so-called 'windmill' on the Oléac ridge when in fact it took place some three kilometres away on the ridge south of Orleix. The originator of this Quixotic error appears to have been the irrepressible Quartermaster William Surtees who describes the French as being *'drawn up on a steep acclivity, near the windmill'*. The eminent historian of the Peninsular War, Sir Charles Oman, accepted the description and it thus became engraved in the historical record. However, after very extensive walking of the ground by the authors it became clear that the description of the ground by the eyewitnesses who had traversed it did not fit with the terrain leading up to the Oléac 'windmill'. Further close reading of the first-hand accounts revealed that no other participant located the action around a windmill. Indeed, Captain Cooke, who was observing the action from the 1st Brigade in close support, states that he *'could see the right of the enemy* [i.e. Villatte's 6th Division] *formed on some heights round a wind-mill two miles to our left.'* [47] Further confirmation comes firstly from the actual nature of the supposed windmill. Had any eyewitness been close to the 'windmill', he would have realised that it was in fact a telegraph relay tower, possibly built on the base of an old windmill, which had been erected in 1793 as part of the Chappe telegraph system designed to facilitate communication along France's southern frontier between Perpignan and Bayonne. Secondly the authors, having conducted extensive searches with metal detectors, discovered no evidence of a fierce firefight around the tower while the heights south of Orleix revealed evidence of an engagement involving Baker rifles. In William Surtees' defence, he was slightly wounded that day and before returning to the fray admitted to *'having swallowed some spirits to remove the faintness'*.[48]

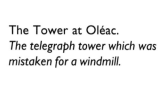

The Tower at Oléac.
The telegraph tower which was mistaken for a windmill.

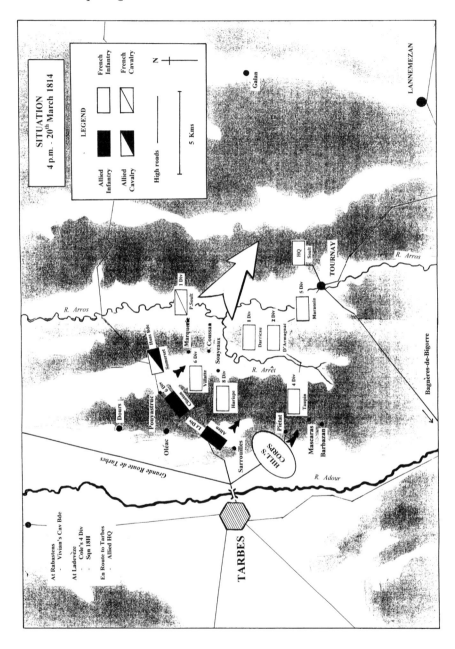

V

The Afternoon of the 20ᵗʰ March – The Pursuit towards Tournay

The French Withdrawal

By now Harispe's and Villatte's Divisions were retreating in some disorder along previously prepared withdrawal routes, some through Boulin in the direction of Sarrouilles and others towards Pouyastruc and Souyeaux, pursued by the Allied 6ᵗʰ Division and the Light Division. Clinton's 6ᵗʰ Division continued to follow up the French withdrawing along the Oléac ridge towards Boulin with its artillery engaging the rear of Villatte's retreating Division. Wellington rode over to speak to Clinton, *"Sir Harry, you have made a very handsome movement."* Clinton bowed as the Commander-in-Chief gazed through his telescope. *"Very well, give them another gun! Show them strong heads of columns and then push them on"*, he ordered.[49]

Apart from these scattered elements of the flank-guard, the remainder of the French army was now well clear of Tarbes itself. On the Tournay route, the leading elements of Darmagnac's and Darricau's Divisions of Comte D'Erlon's Corps together with Maransin's Division under Reille were beginning to establish themselves on the high ground above the Arrêt river-line providing a safe staging post for withdrawing troops. D'Erlon's artillery too had been sited on these heights covering the approach road. Taupin's Division attempted to establish a delaying position at Piétat, which dominated the road from Tarbes to Tournay as it climbed up from the Adour plain.

The Light Division Pursuit

William Surtees found Harispe's 8th Division *'posting away with all expedition to the plain below* [the valley between Orleix and Boulin], *some guns, which had just arrived, giving them an occasional shot, but from which they did not suffer much, they marched away with such rapidity.'* [50] The 95th battalions followed close on their heels and *'had fine rifle practice upon the plain'* [51] while the horse artillery came forward, protected by a squadron of hussars, with the remainder of the division which had followed 2nd Brigade up the hill. By 1.30pm the Light Division had moved off along the ridge with everyone marvelling at the view of Tarbes which *'looked delightful from the heights, surrounded as it was with avenues and gardens, and backed by the lofty Pyrenees'.* [52] They could see Hill's Corps pushing through the town and across the bridge over the Adour, hot on the heels of Taupin's Division as it streamed away up the steep road to Piétat. Cooke described the scene:

> *The town of Tarbes lay in the valley to the right close to the Adour; the dense red columns of our right wing were in the act of passing it with cavalry and artillery; while the glitter of the enemy's bayonets formed a brilliant spectacle, and the tail of their winding columns covered the country, as they rapidly threaded the by-roads through small woods, and over hill and dale. They were also running in a dense crowd on the high road towards Tournay, (threatened by the hussars and horse-artillery) where a rapid interchange of cannon balls took place, and we were in momentary expectation of over-taking them, when broken ground and hedges suddenly*

BOULIN

The Oléac - Boulin Ridge.
Looking south-east from the Orleix ridge towards Boulin. It was across the flat ground here that Harispe's Division withdrew.

intervened, and they eluded our grasp. A French captain stood by the road side imploring for his life, and calling out for the English, in evident fear of the Portuguese and Spanish; he held a commission in his hand, and both his eyes were shot out of their sockets, and hanging on his cheeks!' [53]

The Light Division continued to follow up the retreating French divisions, often in contact with their rear-guard. John Blakiston wondered why Wellington had not ordered a decisive move to cut off the large numbers of stragglers:

'We advanced along the top of the hills towards the eastern side of the town till we arrived near the high-road to St Gaudens, on which the French, who were driven through the town by Sir Rowland Hill, were retreating precipitately – horse, foot, and artillery, pell mell. Why we did not push on I know not; but I think if we had we must have done the enemy some serious injury. As it was we accelerated their pace not a little. I thought, at one time, we were within about a musket shot of their column; but this might have been an optical deception; for we did not offer to molest them.' [54]

The French succeeded in keeping the Rifles at bay with occasional rear-guard actions. But at times the 95th battalions did close with the enemy who were prepared to stand and fight as George Simmons discovered to his cost:

'This day my usual good luck did not attend me, for near the close of day about ninety men threw themselves behind a ditch and kept up a running fire. We were moving upon it to dislodge them when a Frenchman took a long shot at me; the ball fractured my right knee-pan and knocked me down as if I had been struck with a sledge-hammer. Some others, seeing me down, fired several shots at me. My noble servant, Henry Short, as soon as he observed me, came running to me, and, with an oath, observed, "You shall not hit him again but through my body," and deliberately placed himself in front of me. Colonel Barnard rode up, jumped off his horse, and showed me the greatest kindness. I had the pleasure to see the enemy beaten at all points before I left the field of battle, which was a great consolation.' [55]

As the Light Division battalions approached the Tournay road, they could see the French divisions streaming along the high road and adjacent lanes. On occasion the Light Division was in a position to cut off elements of retreating French units. However, the French saw the danger, inclined to their right and, marching with all speed, escaped from their pursuers.

The Allies Follow Up

By 4 o'clock, Hill's Corps had reached the foot of the Piétat hill but was stopped by Taupin's artillery. An attempt by the Allies to cut the Tournay route was made by cavalry who tried to approach from the south along the Barbazon and Mascaras Dessus valleys. This attempt failed as Comte D'Erlon's artillery and troops blocked these approaches. It was about this time that Colonel Vivian's Hussar Brigade arrived at Rabastens from Bordeaux, via Barcelonne and Plaisance, and Lieutenant General Sir Lowry Cole's 4th Division from Bazas and Langon, arrived in the area Ladevèze – Beaumarchés. Both had moved as fast as possible on bad roads, attempting to join the main body of the Allied army. This reinforcement would be welcome but, as events were proving, not essential. On the Allied left, the Light and 6th Divisions had cleared Clauzel's Corps from the Orleix and Oléac ridges, with Freyre's Spanish Division following up in the rear. In the process, Général Pierre Soult's 1st Cavalry Division had been cut off from the French main body and was retreating east well out on the French northern flank. Harispe's and Villatte's Divisions were also retreating piecemeal in an easterly direction not able yet to join up with the remainder of their army on the Tournay road.

Hill eventually gained the high ground around Piétat and was poised to push forward and to take advantage of his gains. However, he became aware of the position which Comte D'Erlon had adopted on the high ground above the Arrêt river which formed the next ridge. Here, two French divisions held a dominating feature and were being reinforced by Taupin's Division as it withdrew and joined them. Infantry and cavalry of Reille's Corps were also in the area in support. It was clear that the French line was far too strong for Hill's Corps alone to attack immediately. To mount an effective assault it would be necessary for Beresford's Corps to concentrate and form part of the line. Soult, by falling back on each ridge-line in turn, had unwittingly exposed himself to considerable danger. Behind the Arrêt river, the Arros river formed another obstacle. If Beresford were able to turn the French northern flank, Soult would be trapped between the two rivers with the bridge at Tournay being the only escape route to Toulouse. Escaping south to Bagnères-de-Bigorre was not an option as it would only lead further into the foothills and narrow valleys of the Pyrenees. Beresford with the 6th Division had gained the heights above Marquerie and Coussan north of the French line but was still not advanced enough to turn the flank and allow a full and coordinated Allied attack to be mounted. The Light Division, which had taken a more south-easterly route from Orleix to Sarrouilles, was now back with the main elements of the Army and was pushed up close to the French held ridge.

Wellington Orders a Halt

It was generally expected that the Commander-in-Chief would order an attack but Wellington was wary of allowing over-enthusiastic troops to conduct pursuits which often became disorganised and vulnerable to counter-attack. Hard lessons had been learnt not least by the 95th at Obidos at the start of the campaign in August 1808 and by the Guards at Talavera a year later. Wellington, however, recognized the strength of the French position with its artillery. He knew that he was not able to form a line and that the French north flank could not be turned before darkness. He was aware that his troops were tired having fought and marched some thirty-five kilometres since 'Rouse' over twelve hours ago. Last Light was now approaching and Wellington had little choice but to call a halt to operations for the day. At 4.45pm he called forward General George Murray, his dependable Quartermaster General. Wellington thought well of him but only as a staff officer, *'He was an excellent subordinate officer, but not fit to be trusted with a great command. His defect was not being able to form troops upon the ground. He could form them very well on paper, but had not the practice enough in the other way.'*[56] Murray had, in the evolution of the general staff during the campaign in Spain, assumed the role of Chief-of-Staff, partly through his own competence and partly because Major Scovell, the code-breaker, was on his staff and thus intelligence had become part of his responsibilities. On the high ground south of Sarrouilles, Wellington gave brief instructions to Murray who wrote them rapidly in his notebook drawn from his sabretache. The Quartermaster General quickly issued the following orders which he handed to the ADCs, who then galloped off to the various commanders:

'Heights near Tarbes, 20th March, 1814, 5pm

Sir Rowland Hill will be so good as to halt the troops under his immediate orders, and place them upon the right of the great road near Angos, and Mascaras, and the other villages farther to the right.

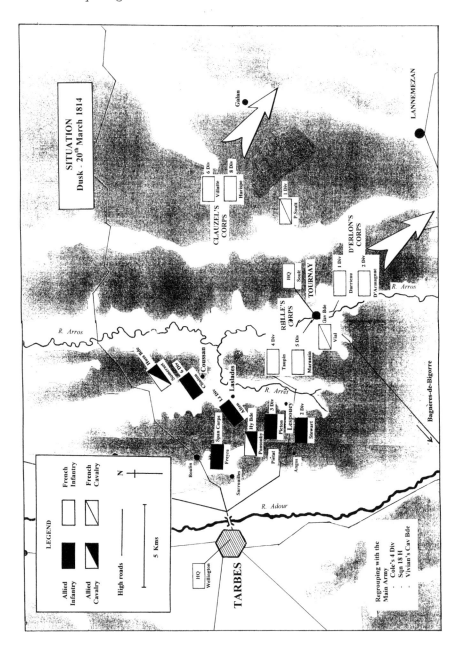

SITUATION
Dusk - 20th March 1814

LEGEND

Allied Infantry

Allied Cavalry

French Infantry

French Cavalry

High roads

5 Kms

N

Wellington HQ

TARBES

R. Adour

Regrouping with the Main Army
- Cole's 4 Div
- Sqn 18 H
- Vivian's Cav Bde

Boulin

Freyre

Sarrouilles

Span Corps

Ponsonby

Hy Bde

Picton

Picat

3 Div

Angos

Stewart

2 Div

Lespouey

Inés Bde

Somerset

Clinton

Coussan

6 Div

Anson

Lasladés

R. Arrêt

RHLLE'S CORPS

Taupin

4 Div

Maransin

5 Div

Vial

Cav Bde

Soult HQ

TOURNAY

R. Arros

1 Div

Darricau

2 Div

D'Armagnac

D'ERLON'S CORPS

R. Arros

CLAUZEL'S CORPS

Villatte

6 Div

Harispe

8 Div

F. Soult

1 Div

Galan

LANNEMEZAN

Bagnères-de-Bigorre

The 3rd Division and Light Division will be on the left of the great road in the neighbourhood of Calavanté, Lespouey, Lansac, and Laslades.

The 3rd Division will be next the great road, and the Light Division more to the left, extending its posts so as to communicate with the 6th Division, which is at Coussan. The cavalry will canton in the villages above mentioned, and the others near which the infantry are directed to encamp.

The Spanish Corps is ordered to canton at Sarrouilles and Boulin.' [57]

Some disagreed with Wellington's decision, feeling that they had the French on the run. General Sir Edward Packenham, the Adjutant General, was reported to be disappointed and annoyed with the failure to continue the pursuit.[58] But Wellington was also thinking ahead on a much broader front and concerned about the French cavalry on Soult's right and possible threats to his lines of communication. He needed more intelligence about French movement on his extreme northern flank and after a brief conversation with Murray, the Quartermaster General, issued a second order:

'Tarbes, 20th March, 1814.

The officer commanding the 7th Hussars will be so good as to send instructions to the squadron of that regiment which was ordered to remain at Nogaro to move forward from thence by Manciet and Vic-Fezensac upon Auch. He will, at the same time, move another squadron of the regiment by Mirande upon Auch. The latter squadron is to be in communication with the army through Rabastens, and also from Mirande by Trie.

The Commanding Officer of the 7th Hussars will be so good as to acknowledge the receipt of this order, and send reports to the Quartermaster-General of the result of the above movements upon Auch.

The Quartermaster-General would be glad to know also whether any late reports have been received from the squadron of the 7th Hussars left at Villeneuve de Marsan.' [59]

Meanwhile, by 6.30pm, the 4th Division had reached Rabastens where they joined Vivian's Hussar Brigade and awaited further orders for the next day's operations.

The Light Division at Dusk

Although it was by now nearly dusk, the riflemen in the 95th battalions still expected an attack to be imminent as the Light

Division's columns closed up to the River Arrêt below the French position where they then came under artillery fire. James Gairdner recorded:

> *The enemy retired to another ridge where they showed great force – the ridge appeared very strong – the 6th Division moved on the extreme right of it & got on it before dark – we were to move down under the foot of it to be ready to attack as soon as the 6th Divn should be sufficiently advanced however night coming on put a stop to our movements & we halted here all night – they showed evident dispositions of retiring before dark however. Just about dark they brought their guns to bear upon us & cannonaded us until it was quite dark. They show scarcely any lights – This is rather a difficult Country he brought us into.'* [60]

As Allied troops moved into their positions for the night, the French took every opportunity to engage those in range with their artillery. However, the firing was not one way and Hardinge's Royal Horse Artillery troop replied *'with my Duck Gun and Switzer* (long 6-pounder and howitzer) *and fired half a dozen long shots and got cover at night.'* [61]

As night fell, the men of the Light Division bivouacked as best they could.

> *'Night came on before arrangements could be made for turning them out of it; and they cannonaded us as we took up our ground opposite them. The*

Major Harry Smith,
95th Rifles.
*Oil painting circa 1840 by
Henry Moseley*

night was cold and dreary; and as the baggage did not arrive, we stretched ourselves on the ground supperless.' [62]

Bivouac areas were allocated and Harry Smith deployed the outlying piquets, one company from each battalion, with numbers of rank and file specified, and exact areas of responsibility delineated. The officers and men had to bed down as best they could, wrapping their 'watch coats' about them. William Surtees' rifleman-servant, believing him to be more seriously wounded had taken his kit to Tarbes where all the wounded were to be sent. Fortunately for Surtees, Major William Balvaird, a company commander, whose servant had managed to bring up his baggage, lent him his tent and bed as he was posted to command the 3rd Battalion's outlying piquet. But, John Blakiston recalls the exhausted and nervous atmosphere in the Division,

'We bivouacked close under the position, which, wrapped in the black mantle of night, looked more formidable than it really was, and which we naturally contemplated with some degree of awe, as destined to be the scene of our conflict next morning. In the course of the night, however, we were relieved from all anxiety on that score by our patrols, who discovered that the enemy had commenced their retreat shortly after dark.' [63]

Casualties of the Day

Total Allied casualties in the two Columns were in the order of 120 wounded and killed, of whom 12 officers and 81 riflemen were from the 95th Rifles. Of the 1st Battalion, Captain Loftus Gray and Lieutenant John Cox were severely wounded and Lieutenant George Simmons less so; two riflemen were killed and five sergeants and 21 riflemen wounded. Captain Duncan of the 2nd Battalion was killed, a sad event which entered the regimental chronicles because of an extraordinary omen. Sir William Cope, a regimental historian, recounts how, when the Rifles were in the Pyrenees, an owl had taken up its quarters with them, and always perched on the tent of Lieutenant Doyle, who was subsequently killed at the Nivelle. Its familiar resting place having gone, it transferred its perch to Captain Duncan's tent. In the rough humour of the camp, it was joked that he must be next on the roster, a joke of which *'he neither liked the point nor saw the wit'*. [64] Lieutenant Colonel Norcott, Captain Miller, and Lieutenant Dixon also of the 2nd Battalion were severely wounded,

Lieutenant Humbley slightly so, and one sergeant and two riflemen killed with fourteen wounded. In the 3rd Battalion, Captain William Cox and Lieutenant Farmer were severely wounded and Lieutenant Sir John Ribton and Quartermaster Surtees less so. One rifleman was killed and three sergeants and 32 riflemen were wounded. The full strength return for the 95th Rifles on 25th March 1814 is shown at Appendix E.

Overall French losses during the day were about double those of the Allies. Using information from A.Martinien's tables of officer casualties[65] and the accepted multiplier of 20 for calculating rank and file casualties, it appears that the French suffered some 230 killed and wounded. Taupin's and Maransin's Divisions both received some 20 casualties each in their defence of Tarbes and the subsequent rear-guard action. Villatte's 6th Division suffered about 85 casualties, probably most from Clinton's artillery fire. Harispe's 8th Division, the opponents of the Light Division, had about 105 casualties in their fierce firefight with the 95th. Although the description of French casualties by the 95th's eyewitnesses involved some inevitable exaggeration, it seems that it was the sheer density of dead and wounded among the vines that struck the observers who were no newcomers to the effects of combat after some six years of fighting.

The 95th's losses are interesting; 12 officers and 81 rank and file show a much higher officer to rank and file ratio than usual. This may have been because of the nature of the ground, a wooded slope ending in a steep convex ridge-top, which would have brought the 95th up close to Harispe's heavy infantry muskets. In addition, rifle regiment officers in a skirmishing line were more vulnerable than line infantry officers protected by three ranks of musket firing soldiers. These casualty figures are not surprising given that normally a successful offensive operation requires a ratio of 3 to1 for attackers against defenders. Here the ratio was reversed with the attacking 95th outnumbered by a force over three times its strength.

The French Consolidate

By 10 o'clock that evening Maréchal Soult had set up his Headquarters in Tournay. Reille's Corps of two divisions was also established on the Lhez ridge just to the west of Tournay with Vial's Brigade of light cavalry. Comte D'Erlon's Corps of two divisions was now bivouacked beyond Tournay. The convoys of field equipment, stores and wounded had been moved on to Lannemezan. Général Pierre Soult's 1st Cavalry Division and Clauzel's Corps of two divisions (Harispe's and Villatte's) had taken their own routes east, well to the north of the high road towards Galan but with a view to swinging south to join up with the main body of the army later on the River Garonne.

At 10 o'clock that night, from his Headquarters in Tournay, Soult wrote to the Ministre de la Guerre.

> 'The Army stayed in position on the hills behind Tarbes occupying the plateau of Oléac and holding posts in front of Tarbes until 11 a.m. Then five or six enemy columns approached. They came from Rabastens, Vic-Bigorre and Villecomptal, always trying to outflank my right. The enemy was expected on all these fronts and the divisions withdrew to Tournay in contact with the enemy. I was very satisfied with the manner in which it was carried out. I saw all the enemy columns. They appeared very numerous. I saw more than 6000 cavalrymen. I deeply regret the necessity of withdrawing to the Garonne and directing the Army to Toulouse. The superior numbers of the enemy is such that I cannot do otherwise without risk of losing the entire Army; nevertheless, I fight every day and I will not leave a position without trying to defend it.' [66]

Soult was also sending instructions ahead to Toulouse for defensive works to be carried out and for the arming and regrouping of local forces.

Wellington's Account of the Day

Wellington returned to Tarbes, where his Headquarters was being established, and after dusk arrived at the house of Comte Antoine Péré, a local senator, in Rue Massey in the centre of Tarbes. Here he received the Préfet and other dignitaries of the town. Meanwhile the Comte's servants rushed to change the sheets on the guest bed which had been occupied on the previous night by a certain Maréchal Soult, the Comte being a very accommodating host!

Later Wellington dictated his dispatch to Earl Bathurst, in which he summarized the day's events:

> 'The enemy retired in the night upon Tarbes. We found them in the morning with the advance posts of their left in the town, and their right upon the

heights near the windmill of Oleac. Their centre and left were retired, the latter being on the heights near Audos [Angos]. We marched in two columns from Vic Bigorre and Rabastens; and I made Lieutenant General Sir Henry Clinton turn and attack the right with the 6th division, through the village of Dours; while Lieutenant General Sir Rowland Hill attacked the town by the high road from Vic Bigorre.

Lieutenant General Sir Henry Clinton's movement was very ably made, and was completely successful. The Light division under Major General C. Baron Alten likewise drove the enemy from the heights above Orleix; and Lieutenant General Sir Rowland Hill having moved through the town and disposed his columns for the attack, the enemy retired in all directions. The enemy's loss was considerable in the attack made by the Light division; ours has not been considerable in any of these operations. Our troops are encamped this night upon the Larret and the Arroz [Rivers l'Arrêt and l'Arros]; Lieutenant General Sir Henry Clinton with the 6th division, and Lieutenant General Sir Stapleton Cotton, with Major General Ponsonby's and Lord Edward Somerset's brigades, being well advanced upon their right.

Entrance to Comte Péré's House, Tarbes.
Wellington rode through these gates on the evening of 20th March. The house has since been demolished.

Although the enemy's opposition has not been of a nature to try the troops, I have had every reason to be satisfied with their conduct in all these affairs, particularly with that of the 3rd division in the attack of the vineyards and town of Vic Bigorre yesterday, and with that of the 6th and Light divisions this day.' [67]

Thus ended Sunday 20th March 1814. In the preceding twenty-four hours the Allies had advanced some thirty-five kilometres from the Vic-en-Bigorre area to the Arrêt and Arros river-lines; much of the advance had been in contact. The French had cleverly avoided a set piece battle, retiring in the same twenty-four hour period from the Vic-en-Bigorre area some forty kilometres to Tournay. They too had been for much of the day in contact yet finally they had broken clean from their enemy to fight another day in circumstances, they hoped, more advantageous to them.

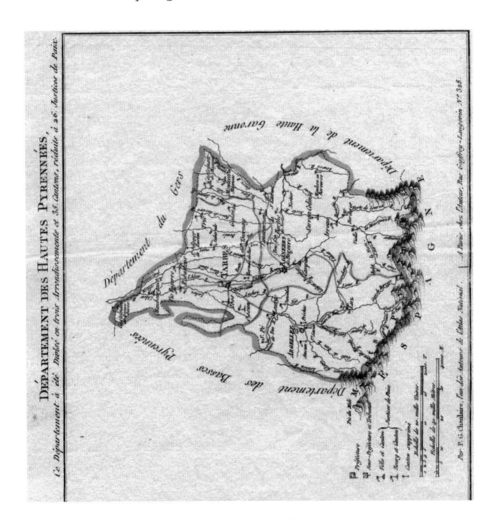

Department of the Hautes-Pyrénées 1802. Typical of area maps available to senior commanders and staff officers.

VI

A Review of Events
of the 20th March

Writing from his Headquarters in Tarbes after the battle on the 20th March, Wellington reported to Earl Bathurst, '*I have had every reason to be satisfied with their* [Allied troops] *conduct.*' This dispatch, when it arrived in London, would no doubt have given the Secretary for War and the Colonies a much appreciated feeling of reassurance and an impression that the actions on the 19th and particularly the 20th, were of no real consequence. A few days later, however, Wellington wrote to Lieutenant General Sir John Hope at Bayonne:

> '*We attacked the enemy's rear guard at Vic Bigorre on the 19th, and we had a partial affair with their whole army at Tarbes on the 20th, and were very near catching them in a terrible situation.*' [68]

General Hope could be forgiven if he had secretly wondered why it was that the French had not actually been caught. Wellington's statement here is tantamount to an admission of disappointment if not failure. One moment he is sending economical messages back to London and the next day admitting to a subordinate that he was unsuccessful in capitalizing on a 'terrible situation' in which the French found themselves.

That same evening, the 20th, Maréchal Soult wrote to his Minister of War deeply regretting, *'the necessity of withdrawing to the Garonne and sending the army to Toulouse. The superior numbers of the enemy is such that I cannot do otherwise without the risk of losing the entire army; nevertheless I fight every day and I will not leave a position without defending it.'* [69]

Clearly, Soult appreciated his vulnerability and the superiority of the Allied army. He felt he had to apologise for retreating. Had Wellington not appreciated his own relative superiority? Had he not fully appreciated the predicament in which Soult found himself? Whatever the answers to these questions might be, it remains an historical fact that on the 20th March 1814, Wellington failed to deliver a *coup de grâce* and curtail if not end the campaign.

The events at Tarbes raise some interesting questions although the answers are not obvious. Armed with the benefit of 190 years' hindsight, it is worth highlighting some of the aspects that hitherto have not been addressed. Since their defeat at Vitoria on the 21st June the previous year, the French had been on the defensive. At a strategic level, they had lost Spain. They had ignominiously been forced back into France and, seemingly, were unable to stop Wellington. St Sebastian and Pamplona had been lost, Bayonne was blockaded and Bordeaux had declared for the King. One cavalry and two infantry divisions had been removed from Soult's Order of Battle and more recently, he had been defeated at Orthez and mauled at Aire.

The principal reason that Wellington continued to pursue Soult once the French had moved back onto French soil was to destroy or neutralize permanently Soult's forces. If Wellington could achieve this, then the menace posed by the 'Army of the Pyrenees' would be removed once and for all. Since the crossing of the Bidassoa in October 1813, Wellington's and Soult's armies had clashed on various occasions. Significant battles had been fought on the Rivers Nivelle and Nive, at St Pierre-d'Irube and at Orthez. Yet, in spite of these contests, Wellington was not able to defeat or neutralize his opponent. Soult had the most remarkable ability to duck and dive and to keep together an under-strength, ill-equipped, and demoralized army. His extremely skilful use of ground also saved him on more than one occasion. It should not be overlooked that Wellington's effective strength also had been reduced with the deployment of two divisions to cover Bayonne and one to Bordeaux. These deployments, however, were from choice.

At Bayonne, Wellington was caught off balance when he allowed his forces to be deployed on both banks of the River Nive. Soult's subsequent attack was dangerous but failed to push home the advantage. At Orthez, Wellington failed to follow up his success and allowed the French to melt away only to regroup once more into an effective fighting force. For the six months leading up to Tarbes, these two massive armies had shunted across the countryside as some giant caterpillar consuming all in their path.

By the time Soult had led and drawn Wellington towards St Sever, it might have been thought that the French plan was to lure the Allied army deep into the interior of France, extend their lines of communications to breaking point, subject them to a partisan guerrilla campaign, and defeat them piecemeal. Their experience in Spain had shown the French the potency of such tactics. However, the civil population was not hostile to the Allies although Soult had tried to incite unrest. In fact, the population was less than enamoured with either the French army or the Imperial cause. The Allies were looked upon as 'deliverers' rather than 'conquerors'.

In March, Soult chose to alter the direction of his retreat by heading south-east towards Maubourguet. If his aim was to head for Toulouse, why did he not head due east from Aire-sur-l'Adour via Vic-Fezénsac, Auch and onto Toulouse? Admittedly, his flanks would have been exposed on this route but no more so than on other routes. As it happened, Soult received instructions at this moment from Napoleon via the Minister of War, stating that the Emperor wished another direction to be pursued and that the campaign be transferred via Pau *'de maniere que vous ayiez toujours votre gauche appuyee aux Pyrénées'*.

Clearly, Napoleon did not want yet another hostile army heading towards Paris nor an army 'liberating' other disaffected towns and cities en route. Napoleon also had in mind that by directing Soult back towards the Pyrenees, there might be the possibility of Soult and Suchet from Catalonia joining forces. Some accounts of the campaign suggest that Wellington drove the French army towards the Pyrenees. This, in fact, does not appear to be the case. Where Soult went, Wellington followed.

Lieutenant George Simmons of the 95th Rifles writing to his parents after being wounded at Tarbes states:

> *'The army that is now opposed to us is Marshal Soult's. He is a very persevering fellow. Though thrashed every time we come into contact with him, still he moves to another position, making it as strong as possible, and waits till we move up and thrash him out of it. The French army fought very obstinately at Orthez, better than usual, but every cock ought to fight better upon its own dung-hill ... however, Soult began to pluck up courage and get very bold, he having drawn us back to the Pyrenees.'* [70]

Sir Thomas Picton's Memoirs reveal also that:

> *'the intentions of the French general were still uncertain; he was continually threatening to give battle to the allies but continually retreated when they came up.   He was drawing Lord Wellington back upon the Pyrenees.'* [71]

These two views, one at divisional level and one at company level, show that it was understood within the army that it was Soult who was doing the pulling to the Pyrenees rather than Wellington doing the pushing.

When Soult withdrew to the general area Lembeye – Maubourguet, he had an opportunity of heading east to Toulouse on the Vic-en-Bigorre to Auch route yet he failed to secure or use this passage. He also failed to secure the Trie-sur-Baïse route to Castelnau-Magnoc which could become another escape direction. Instead, Soult fought a rear-guard action at Vic-en-Bigorre so that he could escape due south to Tarbes. On the face of it, there seems to be no political or military advantage in heading for Tarbes when Soult's declared aim was to seek the security of Toulouse to the east. The French were manoeuvring themselves into a difficult position. By the night of the 19th March, most of Soult's troops were to the west of Tarbes and the Adour and very much in the wrong position for a retreat eastwards.

As the 20th March dawned, the Allied army was poised to advance on two major routes towards the enemy in Tarbes. Wellington chose to divide his army into two columns and advance towards Tarbes with one column on each side of the swollen River Adour. A river running parallel to an advance can be a greater obstacle than one which is at right angles. Wellington had already been caught wrong-footed as he advanced to Bayonne and had elements on either bank of the River Nive. Yet, here again, he was advancing towards the enemy astride a major river with few crossing points. One column could not support the other column if either was attacked. If Soult had realized this error in Wellington's deployment, he could have descended on either column in force and probably routed it before the other column could react. Fortunately for Wellington, Soult was only concentrating on his withdrawal.

As the Allied army set off from Vic and Rabastens towards Tarbes, there seems to have been no clear plan other than to make contact and then react. It must have been obvious that Soult's only option was to withdraw from Tarbes eastwards, yet Wellington made no contingency in his orders for a wider outflanking movement to turn the French flank. Soult, on the other hand, realized that Wellington would probably take the south-easterly route at some stage by cutting across the corner and, therefore, he deployed two divisions and cavalry to block Wellington and to protect the Trie and Tournay roads. When French troops were spotted on the Oléac ridge and the ridge south of Orleix, the 6th Division and the Light Division were ordered to clear the enemy. It is evident that the Allies had no real intelligence as to how Soult had deployed his rear-guard and initially the Allied commitment was piecemeal. In the town of Tarbes, the French withdrew across the bridge over the Adour but then failed to destroy it. This fundamental blunder subsequently allowed Hill's Column to debouch from Tarbes in pursuit

Eventually, the French rear-guards were forced back and they withdrew to the line of the River Arrêt and took up a position with other French troops on the high ground above the river. That evening, Allied forces on the northern flank closed up with the French but, because 6th Division had not turned the French flank, no attack was launched. Blakiston, a battalion commander in 1st Brigade recalled in his memoirs that Wellington appeared to be preparing to attack but he then goes on to say, '*nothing, however, was done*'. Clearly, a hint of disappointment and even criticism can be detected here. As with many of Wellington's regimental commanders, Blakiston was spoiling for a fight and in his opinion, the time was right. About 3 kilometres behind the Arrêt river-line, a second river called the Arros runs parallel to the first. The French had positioned themselves between the two rivers and, had they been attacked and dislodged, their retreat would have been jeopardized by the second obstacle. Here again, a tactical advantage had been lost by the Allies.

That night, Allied patrols discovered that the French had withdrawn lock, stock, and barrel. Soult had achieved a most complicated night manoeuvre of breaking clean with an enemy at his heels. Once more he had extricated his army under the cover of darkness and left the Allies nonplussed. French command and control must have been impressive to effect this withdrawal in darkness and secrecy. Wellington, on the other hand, had ended his day with momentum being lost and the advantages that had been gained during the day being totally dissipated.

Soult now moved with speed and he created both distance and time between himself and the Allied army as he raced towards Toulouse. *'And we were very near catching them in a terrible situation'* suddenly has a contrite ring about it. Soult has to be credited with a masterly manoeuvre which left the humble Allied soldier feeling cheated of a prize which he felt was within his grasp.

It could be argued that the missed opportunity of defeating Soult at Tarbes on the 20th March, prolonged the war. Whatever interpretation is given to the whole episode, there can be no denying the tactical brilliance of the 95th Rifles. Who then won the day? Wellington can hardly be credited with any strategic gain or with any tactical victory. Soult achieved his aim of delaying the Allies for long enough for the French to break clean. In this sense, it was Soult who outwitted the Allies and saved his army.

In overall terms, the general action at Tarbes achieved nothing other than to nudge the French closer to Toulouse. The 20th March is more significant for what it failed to achieve. However, within the context of the engagement as a whole, the action of the three battalion brigade of Rifles remains an outstanding success. The 95th drove a force three times their strength from a vital ridge inflicting many casualties. As one eyewitness recounts:

> *'Certainly I never saw such skirmishers as the 95th... They could do the work much better, and with infinitely less loss, than any other of our best light troops.'* [72]

The 20th March 1814 and the 'Battle of Tarbes' could well have entered the annals as the battle which ended the Peninsular War. Instead, it marks the occasion on which Soult extricated his army before it could be trapped and saved it to fight another day. That day was soon to arrive and it would culminate in Wellington's triumphal entry into Toulouse. However, in the meantime, the Allied response to Soult's escape eastwards was, once more, to follow in his wake.

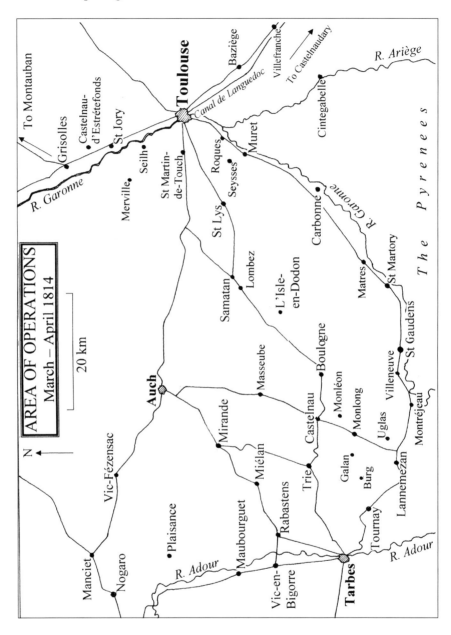

AREA OF OPERATIONS
March – April 1814

20 km

N

VII

Subsequent Events in SW France

A Change of Plan

As dawn broke on Monday 21st March 1814, it became clear to Wellington's troops along the Arrêt river-line that the French had departed during the night. Amongst the soldiers there was doubtless a feeling of both relief and frustration. Once again, the wily Soult had used the cover of darkness to withdraw. By any standard a night withdrawal in secrecy is a particularly difficult operation and Soult had achieved this manoeuvre under the very nose of Wellington. Soult had no time to stop and regroup, and the gathering in of widely dispersed units and individuals had to be effected on the move. Napier explains that night navigation was achieved by lighting fires (beacons) on hills to mark out the general direction to be followed. Field equipment, the wounded, the baggage and stores had been sent ahead and were already on their way to Lannemezan. On the 21st March Soult moved his Headquarters from Tournay to St Gaudens. That evening he reported to the Minister of War:

> 'The divisions under M. le Comte d'Erlon are on the St Gaudens plateau; those commanded by M. le Comte Reille are at Villeneuve-de-Rivière and Bordes [-de-Rivière] and those of M. Le Liut G.al Clauzel with the cavalry of General Soult are at Montréjeau. During the day, the rear-guard was followed only by a detachment of English Light Dragoons.'[73]

Soult's main axis east was towards Toulouse along the route via St Gaudens keeping to the northern bank of the River Garonne. As

Hôpital de l'Ayguerote, Tarbes.
From a design by Baron d'Agos c. 1840. Courtesy of Les Archives Départemental des Hautes-Pyrénées.

Soult explained to Clarke, the Minister of War, he wanted to press ahead and prepare himself without wasting time, '*Je me préparerai sans perte de temps à me reporter en avant.*' [74]

On the 21st March the Allies regrouped and prepared themselves to follow Soult. Wellington realised that the next serious clash with Soult would most likely be at Toulouse. This was a fortified garrison city with a substantial arsenal where Soult could be reinforced by the garrison itself or perhaps by Suchet's troops. If past experience was of any value, Wellington knew that a battle with the French entrenched in and around a fortified city would be bloody and the outcome could not be guaranteed. The defender has all the advantages and is likely to suffer fewer casualties than the attacker. The war in Spain provided ample evidence of this fact while a battle in the open, as at Orthez, would result in a greater loss to the French. Wellington seemed resigned to allowing the French to scuttle off unmolested to the relatively safe haven of Toulouse where they would clearly improve their chances if it came to a pitched battle. No attempt was made to stop the French from bolting to Toulouse and, as will be seen, this failure would subsequently incur a severe penalty.

Clearing the Battlefield

On yesterday's battlefield where the 95th Rifles had so successfully dislodged Harispe's Division, the dead and wounded were collected and moved. Tarbes was a sub-division of the 10e Division Militaire. It not only had the *Hôpital de l'Ayguerote* adjacent to the Cathedral but a temporary military hospital had also been established close by. Some wounded were sent to the temporary hospital whilst those fit enough moved behind the columns on the march. The dead probably had a less than dignified fate. James Anton of the 42nd Highlanders gives an insight into the aftermath of battle:

'We left behind us our dead, our dying, and our wounded; the former careless who shut those eyes that looked up to heaven from their gory bed, or who should consign their naked limbs to a grave in the field of a strange land. But our dying are sometimes left to the mercy of strangers. Shall some good Samaritan bind up their wounds and afford them protection under some hospitable roof, in the country which their invading feet have trod, and while their hands are still reeking with the blood of its harvest defenders? Or shall some sanguinary wretch put an end to their life and pain at once? Perhaps this might be the most welcome to the toil-worn soldier; But, alas! A harder fate awaits many. The midnight plunderer shuts his ears to mercy's call, strips the helpless, bleeding, dying sufferer, and leaves him naked to breathe his last beneath the frosty sky, on the field saturated with his blood.' [75]

After the battle, the women who followed the army, would arrive on the battlefield to look for their loved ones, their husbands and the fathers of their children. If their men were found dead, then their status and means of support was immediately changed and usually for the worse. The women would also tend the other wounded and dying. Prior to 1813, six 'lawful wives of soldiers' to every one hundred men were permitted to accompany a regiment when it embarked for foreign service. This provision was changed by a General Order dated Horse Guards, 10 April 1813 which, henceforth, allowed six wives per company to accompany a regiment when it embarked for active field service. Those wives left behind were granted an allowance to enable them 'to proceed to their Homes, or to the Places at which they intend to reside, during the absence of their Husbands on Service'.

At Tarbes there is no evidence of contempt being shown toward the dead or to the wounded who were nursed locally. In fact the opposite seems to have been the case. Lieutenant George Simmons of the 95th Rifles, who sustained a musket ball wound to his right knee during the action at Orleix on the 20th, states in a letter to his parents written at Tarbes on the 27th March:

> '*On the 21st I was moved on a wagon into this town [Tarbes]. The first person that saluted me was Maud. Judge how delighted I was. [Lieutenant Maud Simmons, George's brother and in the 34th Foot, was appointed Town Major of Tarbes after the battle and was left with elements of his regiment to guard the sick and wounded.] He had got me a comfortable quarter, I had nothing to do but enter it. I have kept my bed until today.*' [76]

In that same letter, George Simmons explains to his parents that:

> '*France is a most delightful country and abounds with everything. The people detest Buonaparte – all but the officers of the army and those others who openly support him and his diabolical cause from interested motives. The people are astonished at the liberality of the English. We behave to them as if we were at home, and, though fighting frequently with Soult's army, in their towns the peaceable inhabitants have more faith in us, generally speaking, than in their own army. This is a happy way of making war, for how many thousands of our brave fellows when wounded and left on the ground would not otherwise have been murdered by the injured peasantry. Instead of that, they take the wounded to their houses, protect and feed them.*' [77]

It would appear that the dead of both armies who fought at Orleix and Oléac were buried in what is known locally as *La Butte des Anglais* or *Le Tombeau des Anglais*. Confusion exists as to the location and precise nature of this burial site but Monsieur Gibaud, a local Orleix historian, notes that '*the last witnesses, very credible, placed the tomb to the east of the Ousse* [the stream running to the east of Orleix] *at the same level as La Heyede.*' [78]

Judge Advocate Larpent recorded in his journal:

> '*Tarbes is a good town and contains a number of good houses. The people received us in general very well, but were quite passive, taking no part in anyway. They had been kept quite in ignorance of all that was going on in the north and at Bordeaux in particular.*' [79]

The Road to Toulouse

Wellington's Headquarters moved from Tarbes to Tournay on the 21st March. Allied reconnaissance was timid and formations advanced with caution. The 95th Rifles followed the French as far as Lannemezan. James Gairdner of the 95th Rifles records in his diary for Monday, 21st March:

'The enemy retired last night. Marched through Tournay to Lannemezan – terribly wild and uncultivated – good cavalry country. The houses in these towns very decent. Rain.' [80]

From Tournay on the 21st March 1814, Wellington issued the following orders for the movement of the Allied army for the 22nd March:

'Lieutenant-General Sir Lowry Cole will move the 4th Division and Colonel Vivians's brigade of cavalry to-morrow morning to Trie, and will communicate from thence with Marshal Beresford at Castelnau, and with head-quarters at Galan.

The 6th Division will move from Bourg to Castelnau.

The hussars and Major-General Ponsonby's brigade of cavalry will also move to Castelnau, and Sir Stapleton Cotton will be so good as to direct one regiment of that cavalry to march with the 6th Division.

After reaching Castelnau, these two brigades of cavalry are to be cantoned in front of that place in such a manner as to extend along the road to Masseube, and along that of Boulogne, to both of which places patroles should be sent. A cavalry post should also be established at Monléon.

The Light Division and Major-General Bock's brigade of cavalry will move from Lannemezan by Uglas and Monlong.

General Freyre will be so good as to put the Spanish corps in motion at 7 a.m., and march by the road which leads from Tournay to Galan, where the corps will receive further directions as to the cantonments it is to occupy.' [81]

Wellington's orders clearly show that his intention was to move the main body of the Army in a north-easterly direction towards Toulouse rather than take the longer route in the wake of Soult along the course of the Garonne. However, Wellington decided to send Hill's Corps after Soult. Separate orders were issued to Hill through the Quartermaster General:

> *'Lord Wellington desires that you will be so good as to put the troops under your immediate orders in motion to morrow morning, and advance by the great road as far as Montréjeau, sending a part of your cavalry more forward, and pushing your patroles as far as you can upon the Toulouse road by St. Gaudens. It is desirable to keep the appearance of the enemy being followed by the main body of the army in that direction.*
>
> *I enclose for your information an extract from the general arrangement, showing what the situation of the rest of the army will be tomorrow. I beg you will keep up a communication from Lannemezan with the centre divisions and Major-General Bock's brigade of cavalry.'* [82]

On the morning of the 22nd March, the Allied army was once more on the move. Soult, however, was well on his way to Toulouse. His forced march over the last twenty-four hours had achieved a clean break between the Allies and the French. Nevertheless, desertion amongst the conscripts was rife, stragglers slowed the pace and, according to French estimates, more than 8000 soldiers had no shoes! Soult used his cavalry to drive on those who were falling behind. The going was difficult, the weather bad, and sickness added to Soult's many problems. During the 22nd March, Soult moved his Headquarters to Martres-Tolosane. The French had marched some eighty kilometres in less than two days while the Allies had advanced a mere fifteen kilometres in the same period.

A French Division on the Move.
Lithograph of Gihaut Frères after Auguste Raffet.

Also on the 22nd, Wellington established his Headquarters at Galan, through which Clauzel's Corps and Harispe's Division had passed the day before. In this period Wellington showed no specific intention to seek engagement. However, at approximately 4pm on the 22nd, Soult's rearguard which was deployed in the area of St Martory was bumped by reconnaissance elements of the 13th Light Dragoons. In London, The Times Newspaper subsequently reported that a dispatch had been received from the Marquess of Wellington, dated Samatan March 25th which stated:

> *'After the affair of the 20th, the enemy had continued to retreat with such rapidity, that the Allies were unable to overtake him excepting on the 22nd, when Major General Fane, with the 13th Light Dragoons, supported by the 3rd Dragoon Guards, charged and pursued them two miles, killing many and taking about 100 prisoners.'* [83]

By the 23rd March, the French had reached the general area Carbonne – Muret. Allied columns were similarly converging on Toulouse, *'Hill is on the great road from St Gaudens; Beresford on that from Auch, and I am between them.'* wrote Wellington.[84] In the wet and cold conditions and with roads in such an appalling state, it was essential that march discipline was maintained within the columns on the move. The baggage element of the column, with its countless mules, was often the cause of delays and hold-ups. A week earlier, from his Headquarters at Viella, Wellington had issued orders for columns on the move. General Officers commanding divisions were to march their columns *'3 men abreast upon all occasions when practicable except when forming to attack an enemy.'* Instructions were given to prevent the baggage impeding progress. A member of the Staff Corps (equivalent to today's combat engineers) was required to be with the baggage and *'soldiers of the Staff Corps are to keep clear on the opposite side of the road a sufficient space for a carriage to pass; this must be done whether the baggage is moving or halting.'* [85]

On the 24th March, the French army arrived at Toulouse exhausted and bedraggled. Incredibly, they had valiantly marched the 150 kilometres from Tarbes to Toulouse in less than four full days and in brutish conditions. The business of providing footwear and other clothing for his troops was high on Soult's list of priorities. However, now he had to prepare himself and his men for what would undoubtedly be a major battle in the days ahead.

Wellington continually moved his Headquarters as he neared Toulouse. He was at Boulogne-sur-Gesse on the 23rd March, at L'Isle-en-Dodon on the 24th, at Samatan on the 25th and at St Lys on the 26th. At the same time, the other columns were closing in. In Tarbes, Lieutenant George Simmons was still convalescing. His letter to his parents written on the 27th, was finished off by his brother Maud when George became too tired to continue:

> *We are well out of the fighting at present, confound it! ... peace must shortly bring us together, when I hope we shall all meet without the loss of legs or arms. I am advising George to go home, but he wishes to see more fighting ... I wish it was possible for you to come and spend few days with us. You would not be a little surprised to see how happy we live in an enemy's country, as they call it, but I think them friends.'* [86]

Major Harry Ross-Lewin of the 32nd Regiment of Foot recalls that in early March, his regiment had been taken out of the line and ordered back to St Jean-de-Luz for new clothing:

> *We reached St Jean-de-Luz in eight days, and, having exchanged our tattered raiments for the new uniforms, set off again on the 18th March to rejoin the army. It rained incessantly as we returned, until, in the seventh day's march, we entered Tarbes; but once arrived there we made ourselves very comfortable.'* [87]

The 32nd Foot was subsequently deployed from Tarbes to Toulouse with the battering train, pontoons and boats. It took this column ten days to reach Toulouse by which time the battle was over.

After recovering from a severe wound, Lieutenant Colonel Augustus Simon Frazer, who commanded the Royal Horse Artillery under Wellington, left St Jean-de-Luz on the 18th March to rejoin Wellington's Headquarters. His journey via Dax, St Sever, Trie, Lombez, St Lys to Seysses took some two weeks and passed through countryside already 'liberated' by the Allies. In various letters written during his journey, Frazer records:

> *'It is evident that Bonaparte is detested ... the people with whom I have conversed all join in expressing detestation of Bonaparte, but frankly avow the fear of speaking their real sentiments ... it is impossible to help remarking that there are no young men to be seen ... we met with several runaway conscripts; I taxed them with being so, they laughed and said "to be sure we are!" ... we passed perhaps twenty horses and mules, which, in different parts of the road, had been suffocated in the mud ... in a room below, they showed us a sick soldier, one of our 18th Hussars, whom they had taken in, we have met before with several similar instances, and in all, the natives*

*have behaved with greatest tenderness and kindness towards our men ... I
never saw a worse bit of road than about a mile of what we have passed,
stiff deep clay up to the horses shoulders.'* [88]

Movement by individuals or groups was relatively safe in the general
area as there was little hostility to the Allies by the civil population.
However, Wellington was particularly clever at communicating with
the civil authorities and he was quite clear in the messages he wished
to promulgate. The method used in this context was to issue
proclamations. Wellington used this means to make known his
requisition requirements and how he expected the general peace to
be maintained. Even at a time when his Headquarters Staff were
preparing for the assault on Toulouse, Wellington issued a proclamation
to all mayors establishing four important Articles (see Appendix C
for the full text of the Proclamation issued on 1 April 1814).

The Battle of Toulouse

Soult had now been in Toulouse a number of days and preparations
for the city's defence were well advanced. Wellington's forces had
converged to the west of the city but unfortunately the River Garonne
lay between the two armies. In addition, the Canal de Languedoc ran
around the city to the north and east creating another and substantial
obstacle. To the east of the city and between the canal and the River
Hers, the Calvinet Ridge dominated any approach to the city from
that direction.

Wellington firstly needed to cross the Garonne. A southerly approach
to Toulouse was deemed particularly difficult as a second river, the
River Ariège, would demand a second river crossing. Wellington,
therefore, decided to cross the Garonne to the north or downstream
from the city. Colonel Frazer had now rejoined Wellington's staff at
Seysses near Muret . In a letter written from the Headquarters on 1ˢᵗ
April, Frazer gives an interesting insight of how a relatively senior
officer perceived the situation:

*'I fully expected this morning that we should have had something to do, but
we have returned from the outposts nearest Toulouse where all is quiet; it is
now 10 o'clock. We were of course out before daybreak. Soult's troops
remained in position on the rising ground beyond Toulouse; as the day
dawned we saw them distinctly enough; there might be some 18,000 or
20,000 men, all infantry. He has probably a division in the town, and is*

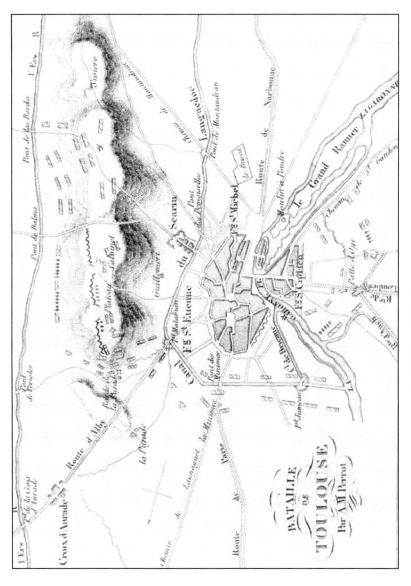

Battle Plan of Toulouse.
Engraved by P. Tardieu after A.M. Perrot.

throwing up intrenchments (which will come to nothing), in front of the
suburb, called St Cyprien, which is on his side of the Garonne. We had
anticipated either an attack or movements on the part of Soult; neither has
taken place; Hill's corps crossed the Garonne yesterday by a pontoon
bridge thrown over the river near Roques , a league from hence. They
marched on the bridge over the Arriège at Cintegabelle, five leagues from
Roques, of which bridge they took possession without opposition. It had
been intended to have taken up the bridge by which Hill crossed, and to
have laid it lower down, just below where the Garonne is joined by the
Arriège. I think this will be still done tonight, and that we shall push
forward to-morrow. We must beat Soult soon, I hope and think; and after
that which way shall we turn?' [89]

Hill's Corps, however, returned to the Garonne's west bank as this
southern approach to the city was deemed unprofitable. An alternative
crossing point had been selected some 18 kilometres downstream
near Merville. On the 4th April, a pontoon bridge was constructed
and by nighfall, Beresford and three infantry divisions, the 3rd, 4th and
6th, with two cavalry brigades and artillery were on the eastern bank.
Harry Smith of the 95th Rifles records:

'These Divisions were strongly posted under Marshal Beresford as a tête du
pont. They were barely established on the opposite side when such a torrent
of rain fell, our bridge could not stem the flood. It was hauled to the shore,
and, of course, our communication cut off. Marshal Beresford had every
reason to apprehend an attack, for the enemy, being in his own country,
possessed perfect information, and would know the moment the bridge was
impassable.' [90]

Wellington crossed the river with some of his staff by boat and
reassured Beresford that an attack was unlikely. Fortunately, Soult
made no demonstration against Beresford's isolated divisions. The
pontoon bridge was rebuilt on the 8th April and the remainder of
Beresford's units crossed to the east bank. The pontoon bridge was
then moved upstream to Seilh. Fortunately a bridge over the River
Hers at Croix d'Aurade had been taken intact and allowed Bereford's
units to swing southwards between the Hers and the Calvinet Ridge.
Hill's Corps was still positioned to the south-west and, in effect,
Toulouse was now surrounded with Allied forces covering the main
approaches. The scene was set for the assault on this heavily defended
fortress city. Wellington's Headquarters, in the meantime, had moved
to St Jory.

In Paris there were momentous developments taking place. News reached Wellington and Soult that the eastern Allies had entered Paris on the 31st March. However, Paris surrendered on the 4th April and Napoleon's Marshals withdrew their support for their Emperor. The Eastern Allies demanded Napoleon's abdication and on the 6th April 1814 he signed the instrument of his abdication. The next day one British and one French messenger left Paris for Toulouse carrying the news of the abdication. Unfortunately, these envoys did not arrive at Toulouse until the 13th April.

As neither Wellington nor Soult had received word that Napoleon had abdicated, the final preparations were made for the forthcoming battle. Wellington's attack opened in the early hours of Easter Sunday, the 10th April. Hill's formations threatened St Cyprien, a suburb on the west bank of the Garonne. On the east bank and to the north, Picton's and Alten's Divisions demonstrated against the canal crossing points, although Picton's impatience had the better of him. He attempted to storm one of the crossings but was repulsed with heavy losses. Wellington had ordered Beresford to move southwards on the west bank of the River Hers until he was in a position to swing west and attack the Calvinet Ridge. This ridge was heavily defended with redoubts and Harispe's and Villattte's Divisions. As Beresford moved south, however, his column became delayed and bogged down and he decided to leave his artillery at the northern end of the Calvinet Ridge where, at least, it could engage the Great Redoubt.

Soult at the Battle of Toulouse – 10th April 1814.
Engraved by Pierre-Eugène Aubert after Joseph Beaume.

The general plan was that when Beresford turned to attack the centre of the Calvinet Ridge, Freyre's two Spanish divisions would attack the northern end. As Beresford's artillery opened fire, the Spaniards attacked. Unfortunately, the artillery was premature and had started its bombardment before Beresford's formations had wheeled to face the ridge. Freyre's divisions took the full force of the French artillery and were forced back with considerable loss. Harry Smith recalled the events as he saw them from the Light Division's position to the north of the Ridge:

> 'I shall only make two or three remarks. Sir Thomas Picton, as usual, attacked when he ought not, and lost men. The Spaniards made three attacks on a very important part of the enemy's position defended by a strong redoubt. The first was a very courageous though unsuccessful attack; the second, a most gallant, heavy, and persevering one, and had my dear old Light Division been pushed forward on the right of the Spaniards in place of remaining inactive, that attack of the Spaniards would have succeeded. I said so at the moment. The third attempt of the Spaniards was naturally, after two such repulses, a very poor one. At this period, about two o'clock in the afternoon, the Duke's staff began to look grave, and all had some little disaster to report to His Grace, who says, "Ha, by God, this won't do; I must try something else." ' [91]

Beresford eventually attained the Ridge on a second attempt with 4th and 6th Divisions and as they moved north along it, the fighting was particularly intense as each redoubt had to be stormed. When Soult realized that he had lost the Ridge, he withdrew his troops back behind the canal and the city walls. It was during this battle that Général Taupin (defender of Tarbes) was killed and Général Harispe (defender of the ridge at Orleix) was severely wounded in the foot.

With the Calvinet Ridge in Allied hands, a short lull ensued while Allied artillery was dragged up the hill and sited. Various minor exchanges took place but dusk brought to an end the day's heavy fighting. The 11th April was relatively quiet. Wellington now dominated the city from the Calvinet Ridge but needed to regroup and redeploy his formations for subsequent operations. The dead had to be buried and the wounded tended. Artillery needed to be repositioned and ammunition and other materiel resupplied. Soult now feared entrapment in the city and concluded that he and the remainder of his army had to escape. At 9pm on the 11th April 1814, Soult withdrew from Toulouse via the bridge at Baziège on the road towards Villefranche-de-Lauragais and Carcassonne. His departure from the city was greeted with relief by the inhabitants of Toulouse. Not only would the city now be saved from heavy artillery bombardment and brutal sacking but civilian casualties would be avoided. Perhaps, therefore, it was fortuitous that an escape route was so readily available! Alternatively, Wellington, who must have known that Napoleon would soon be toppled, could have sealed Toulouse and imprisoned the French army until peace was declared.

In Toulouse, some 1600 wounded and quantities of guns and stores were abandoned by the withdrawing French army. The wounded included three generals. Casualties on both sides were heavy. Fighting had been fierce and bloody and had resulted in 4500 Allied and 3200 French casualties. These figures must reflect the fact that the Allies failed to stop Soult at Tarbes. It was a heavy price to pay. The figures are also poignant because the battle could have been avoided if the news of Napoleon's abdication had arrived in time. In comparing casualty figures, the French inflicted more casualties on the Allies. This fact and other spurious arguments were subsequently used by the French to present Toulouse as a French victory. Soult, once again however, retreated under the cover of darkness possibly to link up with Suchet and to fight yet another day. Interestingly, Suchet was to write later that neither should nor could he have come to the aid of Soult at Toulouse. Wellington may have failed to destroy Soult's army at Toulouse but the chief city in South West France was now in Allied hands.

The political sands were fast running out and Soult had few options left open now that news of the Allied entry into Paris had been received. He had originally intended to hold Toulouse at all costs but he had confided to Suchet that, if he was forced to abandon Toulouse, he would head north for Montauban on the high road to Paris. As it was, Soult escaped south towards Villefranche and Castelnaudray, not far from his birthplace, St Amans-Labastide near Mazamet. He was in effect 'heading home' after a last attempt to defend the land of his birth.

As the 12th April dawned, Soult was well on his way and no serious attempt was made to stop him. At around 10am, Wellington entered Toulouse in triumph and although a welcoming party of city officials was there to greet him, the Allied Commander-in-Chief somehow missed them and entered the city unnoticed. Toulouse had declared for the King and the white cockade was to be seen everywhere. John

Wellington's Entry into Toulouse – 12ᵗʰ April 1814.
Engraved by T. Fielding after R. Westall R.A.

Meyricke wrote to his father: *'next morning [the 12ᵗʰ] the Division were sent into houses in the suburbs, my house was rather airey being full of loop-holes. I went into the Town where the white flag was flying on the Town Hall and the bust of Bonaparte thrown out of the window – everybody appeared in high spirits.'* [92] That evening, as Wellington was changing for dinner, Lieutenant-Colonel Hon Frederick Ponsonby, sent by the Commander of the 7ᵗʰ Division, arrived from Bordeaux with the news that Napoleon had abdicated. Three hours later, the two envoys from Paris arrived with the official news. Wellington was quick to send on Colonels Cooke and St Simon to Maréchal Soult. The official news caught up with Soult on the 13ᵗʰ April near Villefranche. He chose not to accept the authenticity of the communiqué then and there. However, a few days later Soult received confirmation from Maréchal Berthier who had changed loyalty to the new Provisional Government. The news was also sent to Suchet and he and Soult both agreed to an armistice with the Allies. Although elements of the Allied army had followed the French as far as Villefranche, a formal demarcation line was now drawn up between the two armies. War was at an end. Toulouse was *en fête* and celebrating. Soldiers were 'stood down' and relaxing while thoughts began of returning home. Thoughts also, not unreasonably, turned to pay as both officers and men were nine months in arrears!

Bayonne

The French garrison at Bayonne of some 14,000 men and governed by Général Pierre Thouvenot, was still blockaded by the 1st and 5th Divisions under the command of Sir John Hope and had been for the last six moths. Hope had some 8000 well equipped men who were suitably deployed around Bayonne. The blockade was effective and there was little activity between the two forces. There appeared to be no good reason for a high state of readiness. Although news had reached Bordeaux and Toulouse of Napoleon's abdication, Thouvenot decided stubbornly to hold out at Bayonne and not surrender. He had been informed of the abdication but refused to accept the news. Possibly from spite or from sheer belligerence, Thouvenot launched a dramatic sortie of some 6000 men against the Allies during the night of the 14th April. The Allies were taken by complete surprise. Fighting was fierce, confused and the French took the village of St Étienne. General Sir John Hope was taken prisoner and Major General Andrew Hay, Commander 5th Division, was killed. It was not until around dawn that the Allies counter-attacked and drove the French back into the Citadel.

Daylight on the 15th April revealed the cost of this pointless French sally. French casualties amounted to just over 900 while the Allies suffered some 600 casualties. However, Bayonne finally surrendered on the 27th April when Thouvenot received formal notification of the general situation and a copy of the armistice of the 17th April. This needless attack by the garrison of Bayonne was a particularly loathsome and bloody footnote to a war which had technically already ended. In the specific political and military context of April 1814, the sortie from Bayonne will always be remembered as an example of the stupidity and arrogance of one Napoleonic commander.

Peace and Withdrawal

Soult's Army of the Pyrenees and Suchet's Army of the South finally came together to form a royalist army in the south of France under the command of Suchet. The Allied army in and around Toulouse was still well over 45,000 men including many wounded. The logistical problems were immense. Troops were billeted over a wide area and accommodated with local families where possible.

On the 27th April, Louis-Antoine de Bourbon, Duc d'Angoulême, the nephew of Louis XVIII and the leader of the Bourbon movement, was greeted by Wellington outside Toulouse. Colonel Frazer recalls the event:

'About 2, Lord Wellington, attended by his general officers and all head-quarters in their gayest costume, rode out to meet the Duc d'Angoulême; the meeting took place about two leagues from Toulouse on the Auch road, a little beyond the village of St. Martin du Touch. On going out one could hardly get along; it was impossible, in passing the crowds, not to contemplate the passing scene, and to contrast it with the far different ones of which almost every step reminded us. Near St. Martin was to have been our field of action had Soult attacked us before we crossed the Garonne... The

Garde Urbaine (or national troops of Toulouse), which had been formed on the esplanade near the Porte de Ste. Catherine at the entrance of the suburb, filed after the procession, keeping abreast of the Duke. One could not but smile as their bayonets crossed, but not in strife, with those of the English troops... To describe the enthusiasm is impossible, the silent

Louis XVIII. *Published by Furne, Jouvet et Cie.*

Louis-Antoine, Duc d'Angoulême. *Engraved by Benoist after Kinson.*

gaze of many, the wild tumultuous joy of others, and the cheers of acclamation
which occasionally burst from all – "Vive le Roi!" "Vivent les Anglais!"
"Vivent nos Libérateurs!" "Vive Lord Wellington!" and then, as if the
Duke had been for a moment forgotten, "Vive le Duc d'Angoulême!"
"Vive le Fils de Henri Quatre!" Shakespeare would describe such a scene:
I cannot.'[93]

Colonel Frazer also recalls meeting Monsieur de Kerboux, ADC to
the new Minister of War, Général Pierre Dupont. Kerboux told
Frazer that he was on his way to *'direct Suchet to assume the chief command*
of Soult's army as well as of his own, and to order Soult to Paris to give an
account of his conduct'. Kerboux indicated that he was convinced that
Soult was well aware of the events in Paris prior to the Battle of
Toulouse. Kerboux also wanted to know whether Wellington knew
of the events. Frazer replied that *'we were convinced his Lordship did not; it*
was impossible.'[94]

The next evening there was a Grand Ball held in the Capitol in the
centre of Toulouse to celebrate the Peace and each Allied regiment

received two invitations. Harry Ross-Lewin attended and recalls the celebrations:

> '*At ten martial music announced the arrival of Lord Wellington, at the great stair case; and on his approach, accompanied by the mayor of Toulouse, the company rose, and formed a lane, through which he passed to the octagon room, the last of the suite. Here the royal throne was placed under the picture of Louis XVIII, and on one side a seat was prepared for the British commander, over which his portrait was in like manner suspended... The concert ended with "God Save the King," in full chorus... Waltzes and other dances then commenced; and really, any spectator of the scene, who did not call to mind the innate levity and volatility of the French, would with difficulty have been able to persuade himself of the fact, that those dancers, who were merrily spinning and swimming through those gaily-decked apartments, had so recently beheld their territory violated, their troops vanquished, and their national pride humiliated, by the very men to whom this entertainment was given. However, I feel bound to add, that I did not see there a single officer belonging to the regular army of France.*' [95]

The Capitol, Toulouse

Although Ross-Lewin recalls seeing no French officers at the Ball, Colonel Frazer mentions that *'the only French General who waited yesterday upon the Duc d' Angoulême, was Count Clauzel, a pleasing looking man; the count had previously paid a visit to Lord Wellington.'* [96]

The day following the Ball, the 6th Division left Toulouse and marched to Auch. The Light Division and the 95th Rifles marched north and the three battalions moved into cantonments at Castelsarrasin near Moissac on the River Tarn, Castelnau d'Estrétefonds, and Grisolles, both on the River Garonne. Here they were well received by their hosts and enjoyed the relaxed atmosphere and warm weather. Other divisions moved out of Toulouse as a general movement to Bordeaux was put into effect. On the 1st June, the 95th strapped on their equipment, crossed the Garonne, and set off on foot for Bordeaux which was reached 15 days later, having marched the 250 kilometres from Toulouse via Lectoure and Condom. At Bordeaux, the three battalions of the 95th Rifles encamped near Blanquefort just to the north of the city where they remained for three weeks prior to being called forward for embarkation. Others had sailed down the Garonne. British, Portuguese, Spanish and camp followers were all on the move. During May and June, the British troops assembled at Bordeaux while the Spaniards headed home across the Pyrenees. Commissary Augustus Schaumann records:

> *'On our way we passed several Spanish regiments which were being sent back home. They made a dreadful tumult as they marched along. Their hatred of the English, and particularly of Lord Wellington, who had them hanged whenever they robbed or were guilty of disobedience, manifested itself even towards me as I turned aside and halted to let them march by. They used insolent language, made threatening gestures with their bayonets, insulting my men, and seemed quite disposed to plunder my baggage. This behaviour, which, with my pistols clasped in my hands, I could only encounter with the most contemptuous of looks, was allowed to continue without the smallest reproof from the Spanish officers, who did not dare to open their mouths, but, looking a little shamefaced, slunk by in a state of complete apathy. One of these regiments had a drum-major who was wearing the complete ceremonial uniform of Marshal Soult, which had been taken at Vitoria.'* [97]

At Bordeaux there was intense activity as the army prepared itself to embark. As the 95th marched through Bordeaux, the battalions were reviewed by Wellington who was saluted with loud cheers. Transports were sailed up the Garonne and points of embarkation were at sites along the river. The 1st and 2nd Battalions of the 95th embarked on *HMS Ville de Paris* and on the 8th July the 3rd Battalion embarked on *HMS Dublin*, reaching Plymouth ten days later and marched with the band playing to their barracks. Schaumann records that he sailed down the Garonne to Pauillac where he spent a week:

> *'Suddenly orders came along commanding all officers and men of the English army quartered in Bordeaux to leave the place immediately, and I was obliged to go. It was exceedingly difficult to sell either horses or mules in the town, for the whole of the army passing through for embarkation, especially the infantry, had got rid of all their riding horses, mules and donkeys at any price they could get for them. Thus every stable in Bordeaux was packed full, and nobody wanted to buy... on the afternoon of the 4th July, 1814, my brother Edward and I got into a boat with our luggage in order to find our ship which was lying in the roads. When we were taken on board, we were surprised to find the deck was so completely occupied by passengers, wrapped in blankets, who had already retired for the night, and the cabin, the berths, and the whole ship so hopelessly crowded with officers, servants, invalids, women, children and luggage (even Lord Wellington's pack of hounds and a number of horses were on board), that for a while we could find no room whatever.'* [98]

Bordeaux and the points of embarkation witnessed many tragic and harrowing farewells. Soldiers had to abandon those Portuguese and Spanish womenfolk who had attended them and the Army faithfully throughout the campaign. Many had to part from wives and from children. The camp followers were simply left behind to fend for themselves and to find their own way home. The Portuguese troops embarked for Lisbon, British infantry for England, Ireland, Canada, America and the West Indies. The cavalry and other horse units started their long march from Toulouse to the Channel ports. Not only was this experienced and hardened army withdrawing from its theatre of operations, it was also in the process of being dismantled.

Wellington left for Paris at the end of April. He *'rode a white horse into Paris on the 4th May, in time for the parade of Allied troops before Louis XVIII, having been gazetted Duke of Wellington on the 3rd May 1814.'* [99] From Paris, Wellington went on to Madrid and then returned to Bordeaux where he reviewed his troops and on the 14th June, he issued his final and farewell Order. He called again at Paris and then, on the 23rd June 1814, he landed at Dover to a hero's welcome.

Over the coming months, the Allied army left France but leaving in its wake, the inevitable trail of sadness, destruction and debris. Perhaps out of this debris, the good reputation of the British remained intact. It would, however, be necessary once again to field an Allied army against Napoleon. Waterloo was less than twelve months hence and many of the regiments dispersed in the Spring and early Summer of 1814 would find themselves again on Continental soil.

The Peninsular War was a conflict which involved many fierce and bloody battles. The 95th Rifles were involved in most of them and their Battle Honours reflect their outstanding contribution. 'Tarbes' was never granted as a Battle Honour yet the ferocity of the action on the 20th March 1814 was never forgotten. Years later, Wellington, when asked which was the 'sharpest fight' at which he had been present, replied,

"That near Tarbes."[100]

Postscript

The dislodgement of the French from Tarbes by the Allies on the 20th March 1814 was, in itself, no great military achievement. Even before the Columns of Hill and Beresford had made contact with the French, Soult had decided to withdraw east to Toulouse. Soult's plan involved the deployment of two divisions as a rear-guard on the ridges of Oléac and Orleix to the north-east of Tarbes. Villatte's 6th Division and Harispe's 8th Division were ordered to hold back the Allies whilst the French army withdrew from Tarbes itself and, if possible, to keep open the Tarbes – Trie-sur-Baïse road.

From the outset, this French rear-guard had an imperative role to play in the French withdrawal plan. Général Clauzel, the rear-guard corps commander, would not have approached his mission other than with the utmost determination. Clauzel's force was formidable by any standard and his two divisions were supported by Général Pierre Soult's 1st Cavalry Division deployed on the Tarbes-Trie road.

When Wellington ordered the French to be cleared from the Orleix ridge, he could not have known the true strength or nature of the French dispositions. Consequently, Colonel Barnard who commanded the Light Division's 2nd Brigade, initially only committed the 2nd Battalion 95th Rifles. Very quickly, however, this battalion sized skirmishing line soon involved all three 95th battalions in a pitched battle against Harispe's 8th Division of some 4500 men who were deployed on vital high ground of their own choosing. Not only were the numerical and topographical odds heavily stacked against the riflemen of the 95th battalions, but the French were clearly determined to hold their ground, certainly until the rest of the French army had withdrawn.

Initially, the riflemen of the 95th skirmished their way to their objectives but then the battle became more conventional. Général Harispe launched three successive counter-attacks against 2nd Brigade yet failed to stem the advance. The French were driven from their positions and forced to flee. Wellington recognised that the 95th action was an outstanding achievement and his remark about the 'sharpest fight' at which he had been present confirms his opinion of the affair. His comment to Barnard about the 'destructive power of your Rifles' equally acknowledges the skill and effectiveness of the 95th.

At battalion level, even such hardened and experienced men as William Surtees recalled that *'we got within a hundred paces of this formidable body, firing from which was the hottest I had ever been in, except perhaps Barossa'*. When, however, it came to describing the day's events in his Dispatch, typically Wellington was unable to express specific praise for the 95th, *'I have had every reason to be satisfied with (our troops') conduct …particularly with that of the 6th and Light Divisions this day; … The enemy's loss was considerable in the attack made by the Light Division.'* This somewhat economical account, without mentioning the 95th Rifles by name, hardly matched their hard won fight against overwhelming odds of 3 to 1. The 95th Rifles lost 93 killed and wounded, amongst whom were one officer killed and eleven officers wounded, while Harispe's Division sustained even more casualties with a high proportion killed. For the riflemen, the fighting that day on the ridge was quite a battle.

John Blakiston, who served with the Portuguese battalion in the Light Division, wrote about the riflemen of the 95th, *'They possessed an individual boldness, a mutual understanding, and a quickness of eye in taking advantage of the ground, which taken altogether, I never saw equalled. They were in fact as much superior to the French Voltigeurs as the latter were to our skirmishers in general. As our Regiment was often employed in supporting them, I think I am fairly qualified to speak of their merits.'* [101]

After arriving back in England in 1814 from France, the 1st and 2nd Battalions of the 95th deployed to Belgium in 1815 and fought at Waterloo. Only elements of the 3rd Battalion fought at Waterloo as five companies had already been deployed to America. In 1816, the 95th Rifles was reconstituted as an independent Corps and designated

'The Rifle Brigade'. In 1966, the Rifle Brigade joined the King's Royal Rifle Corps, its sister regiment, and the 43rd & 52nd Light Infantry, with which it had formed the Light Division in the Peninsula, to become the Royal Green Jackets. The Regiment has now joined the Light Infantry and other regiments to form The Rifles, a name drawing much from the annals of Wellington's army.

It is not within the limited scope of this book to explore the convoluted topic of Peninsular War battle honours, medals and clasps. Suffice it to say that, for this period, the subject is rife with anomalies and contradictions. Guidelines governing awards appear to be far less than precise. For the period 1813-1814 covered here, the following battle honours were approved: Pyrenees, St Sebastian, Nivelle, Nive, Orthez, Toulouse and Peninsula. The 95th Rifles were granted all these honours except St Sebastian. However, no such honour was given or claimed for Tarbes yet here was a dramatic battle involving exclusively the brigaded three battalions of one regiment. Losses by the 95th at Tarbes were greater than the losses suffered by them at any of the other actions in 1814 for which the Regiment was honoured. As Sir Harry Smith wrote in his Autobiography when referring to the Light Division at the Battle of Toulouse, '...*until the afternoon we literally had done rather worse than nothing.*' 95th casualties at Toulouse are usually quoted as 10 killed and 76 wounded, less than the total at Tarbes. The Regiment was granted the honour 'Toulouse' but 'Tarbes' seems to have been passed over.

Officers were entitled to receive the Army Gold Medal with clasps. However, it was not until 1847 that approval was given for a 'Military General Service Medal 1793-1814' for all ranks. This medal had twenty nine clasps covering the Peninsular War and other theatres of operation and conflicts. Individuals were required to submit personal applications for this medal, which was then issued in 1848. Twenty-one of the clasps covered the battles of the Peninsular War including those in France for which battle honours had already been granted. 'Tarbes' therefore, was not identified by a separate clasp. In passing, it is worth noting that of only eleven individuals who received fourteen clasps, one was Sergeant Joseph Hindle of the 95th Rifles. Any case for a 'Tarbes' clasp would therefore probably be dependent on the issue of an appropriate battle honour being resolved.

It was not until 1838 that the 95th Rifles, by now the Rifle Brigade, met face to face with Maréchal Soult himself. He had been sent by

King Louis-Philippe as his special representative to the Coronation of the young Queen Victoria. A few days later the Rifle Brigade marched from its quarters to the Tower of London where it was inspected by its Colonel-in-Chief, the Duke of Wellington, accompanied by his old opponent Soult. Wellington and Soult had become acquainted with each other many years earlier in Paris when Wellington was the British ambassador. It was for this and other good reasons that Soult had been chosen to represent France in London.

A study of early 19th Century French maps and cadastral plans show that today the ground over which the action at and around Tarbes took place is virtually unchanged. Fields, vineyards, woods, streams, roads, and tracks are the same today as they were in 1814. The landscape of the battle area has been neither spoilt nor obliterated by urban development and a visit to the area is both evocative and rewarding. Sadly, there is no field marker, French or British, which identifies the battlefield or commemorates those of both sides who lost their lives. No recognition is given to either regiment or man. Today *randonneurs* enjoy the area and walk the Orleix and Oléac ridges without any knowledge of what happened on the 20th March 1814. Surely there is a case to be answered here!

A guide to a suggested tour of the battlefield is at Appendix F.

APPENDIX A

Timetable – 20th March 1814

A soldier's day in Wellington's army was long and exhausting as the following timetable for the 20th March 1814 illustrates. By 7pm on the 19th March, after a long march, most regiments halted. Although an hour after dusk, soldiers then cooked a meagre meal as best they could, prepared their equipment for the next day, and finally bedded down for the night. Some had to go out on piquet or patrol duty. An average night's sleep was about five hours. After their approach march, the 95th Rifles bivouacked in and around the farms and barns of Haget. Wellington's orders for the next day had already been issued which specified the start time for the next morning.

The timetable below focuses mainly on the Light Division and the 95th Rifles, which during the day marched some thirty-five kilometres as well as fighting their way along the Orleix ridge. The timetable is constructed from known events, Standing Orders for the Division, and time and distance calculations. It should be remembered that 'roads' were no more than rough tracks and the 95th Rifles had to fight over open hilly country in their battle with the French.

3am	Brigade Major orders preparatory bugle call which is repeated by Commanding Officers' buglers of each battalion.
3.15am	1st Bugle Call. Breakfast, water & feed horses, strike camp.
4.15am	2nd Bugle Call sounds 'Rouse'. Companies turn out on parade and are joined by guards and inlying piquets.

4.30am	3rd Bugle Call sounds 'Assembly'. Captains march companies to regimental assembly points and baggage is centralised by regiments.
4.45am	4th Bugle Call sounds 'Advance'. 95th move during darkness from Haget to assembly area at Rabastens.
5.20am	First Light
7.15am	Right and Left Columns ready to move on Tarbes. French troops start to withdraw from Tarbes and their rear-guard deploys to Orleix-Oléac area.
7.30am	Columns leave Vic and Rabastens. Light Division heads south towards Tarbes along the high road at approx. 4kph.
10am	6th Division leaves the Column to begin flanking movement.
11am	French rear- and flank-guards in position. Other French troops continue to withdraw east.
11.30am	Left Column with Light Division in the lead arrives general area opposite Orleix. French piquet spotted. One company of 2nd Battalion 95th sent to probe position.
11.45am	All three battalions of 95th committed. 6th Division with cavalry support moves up via Dours onto the Oléac ridge.
12 noon	95th main action begins.
1pm	95th drive the French 8th Division from the Orleix ridge. 6th Division forces French 6th Division to withdraw from the Oléac ridge.
1pm-2pm	Light Division and 6th Division pursue French towards Boulin.
2pm	Hill's Column moves through Tarbes and across the Adour. French continue to retreat eastwards.
2pm-4.30pm	Allies advance east in pursuit of French. Hill's troops reach foot of Piétat hill by 4pm. Cole's 4th Division arrives at Ladevèze-Beaumarchés and Vivian's cavalry reaches Rabastens.
4.30pm	Allied divisions reach the Arrêt river-line. 6th Division fails to turn the French northern flank.
5pm	Wellington orders a general halt.
6.15pm	Last Light. French artillery harasses the Allied forward positions.

6.30pm-8pm   Piquet and patrols deployed. Troops bivouac. 4ᵗʰ
Division reaches Rabastens by 6.30pm. Wellington
moves back to Tarbes and Comte Péré's house.

8pm- midnight French withdraw throughout the night. By 10pm
Soult establishes his Headquarters at Tournay.

Signals of the Bugle Horn in the Movements of Light Troops.
From Rottenburg's 'Regulations for Riflemen'.

APPENDIX B

Orders of Battle – 20th March 1814

The detailed composition of the Allied and French armies on the 20th March 1814 is not recorded as such. Therefore the outline Orders of Battle shown below have been gleaned from Operational Orders, witness statements, Standing Orders, Regimental histories, Army lists, and various French accounts. The principle of 'best evidence' has been used throughout. Additional detail has been provided here only on those organisations featured in the text.

ALLIED ARMY

Commander-in-Chief – Field Marshal Sir Arthur Wellesley, Marquess of Wellington

Headquarters

Adjutant General – Maj Gen Sir Edward Packenham

Quartermaster General – Maj Gen Sir George Murray

Military Secretary, Commander Royal Artillery,

Chief Engineer, Civil Staff

Left Corps

Corps Commander – Lt Gen Sir William Carr Beresford

<u>Cavalry</u> – Lt Gen Sir Stapleton Cotton

Light (Hussar) Brigade – Maj Gen Lord Edward Somerset
 7th Hussars (Squadrons deployed on long range reconnaissance)
 10th Hussars
 15th Hussars

Heavy (Dragoon) Brigade – Col Lord Charles Manners*
 3rd Dragoons
 4th Dragoons
 5th Dragoon Guards

<u>Artillery</u>

E Troop Royal Horse Artillery

Other Artillery Units

<u>6th Division</u> – Lt Gen Sir Henry Clinton
1st Brigade – Maj Gen Pack (three battalions)
2nd Brigade – Maj Gen Lambert (four battalions)
Portuguese Brigade – Maj Gen Douglas (three battalions)

<u>Light Division</u> – Maj Gen Charles, Baron von Alten

1st Brigade – Maj Gen Kempt
 1st Bn 43rd Light Infantry
 1st Bn 52nd Light Infantry
 3rd Bn Caçadores (Portuguese Light Infantry)

2nd Brigade – Col Barnard
 1st Bn 95th Rifles – Lt Col Ross strength 560
 2nd Bn 95th Rifles – Lt Col Norcott 600
 3rd Bn 95th Rifles – Lt Col Gilmour 555

<u>Spanish Corps</u> – Gen Don Manuel Freyre
Marcilla's Division
Espeleta's Division

Right Corps

Corps Commander – Lt Gen Sir Rowland Hill

<u>Cavalry†</u>

Light (Light Dragoon) Brigade – Maj Gen Henry Fane
  13ᵗʰ Light Dragoons
  14ᵗʰ Light Dragoons

Heavy (Dragoon) Brigade – Col Johann Baron von Bülow‡
  1ˢᵗ Dragoons KGL
  2ⁿᵈ Dragoons KGL

Heavy (Dragoon) Brigade – Col Arthur Clifton
  1ˢᵗ Royal Dragoons
  3ʳᵈ Dragoon Guards

<u>Artillery</u>

<u>2ⁿᵈ Division</u> – Lt Gen Sir William Stewart
  1ˢᵗ Brigade – Maj Gen Barnes
  2ⁿᵈ Brigade – Maj Gen Byng
  3ʳᵈ Brigade – Maj Gen O'Callaghan
  Portuguese Brigade – Maj Gen Harding

<u>3ʳᵈ Division</u> – Lt Gen Sir Thomas Picton
  1ˢᵗ Brigade – Maj Gen Brisbane
  2ⁿᵈ Brigade – Maj Gen Keane
  Portuguese Brigade – Maj Gen Powers

<u>Portuguese Division</u> – Maj Gen Le Cor
  1ˢᵗ Brigade – Maj Gen Da Costa
  2ⁿᵈ Brigade – Maj Gen Buchan

<u>Morillo's Spanish Brigade#</u> (three battalions)

Recently Arrived From Bordeaux

Light (Hussar) Brigade – Col Sir Richard Vivian
　　18th Hussars
　　1st Hussars KGL

4th Division – Lt Gen Sir Lowry Cole
　　1st Brigade　–　Maj Gen Anson
　　2nd Brigade　–　Maj Gen Ross
　　Portuguese Brigade – Gen Vasconcello

Detached

1st and 5th Divisons at Bayonne under Lt Gen Sir John Hope

7th Division at Bordeaux commanded by Lt Gen George Ramsay

Notes

The following notes are compiled from Sir Charles Oman's 'History of the Peninsular War Volume VII (Clarendon 1930).

*Usually referred to as Ponsonby's Heavy Cavalry Brigade, it was temporarily commanded by Col Lord Charles Manners while Maj Gen Hon William Ponsonby was absent on leave.

†Wellington was also reinforced in early March by Maj Gen Terence O'Loghlin's Heavy (Household) Brigade and five regiments of Portuguese cavalry. These regiments are, however, not mentioned in the text as taking part in the events associated with the action at Tarbes and have therefore been omitted from the detailed ORBAT.

‡Col Johann von Bülow had assumed command of Bock's Heavy Cavalry Brigade as Bock had been drowned at sea in February en route to Germany.

#Morillo detached three battalions from his Division at Navarrenx and placed them under Hill's command while he himself stayed at Navarrenx with his remaining three battalions.

L'ARMÉE DES PYRÉNÉES

Commandant en Chef – Maréchal Nicolas Jean de Dieu Soult, Duc de Dalmatie

État-Major Général

Chef de l'État-major général, Adjudant-commandant,

Commandant l'Artillerie, Commandant de Génie

Division de Cavalerie – Gén Baron Pierre Benoît Soult

> Brigade – Gén Baron Jean-Baptiste Berton
> 2e Hussards
> 13e Chasseurs
> 21e Chasseurs

> Brigade – Gén Baron Jacques Laurent Vial
> 5e Chasseurs
> 10e Chasseurs
> 15e Chasseurs
> 22e Chasseurs

Corps Reille – Aile Droit – Lt gén Comte Honoré Charles Reille
> 4e Division – Gén Baron Eloi Charlemagne Taupin (two brigades)
> 5e Division – Gén Baron Jean-Pierre Maransin (two brigades)

Corps D'Erlon – Centre – Lt gén Jean-Baptiste Drouet, Comte d'Erlon
> 1re Division – Gén Baron Augustin Darricau (two brigades)
> 2e Division – Gén Baron Jean-Barthélemy Darmagnac (two brigades)

Corps Clauzel – Aile Gauche – Lt gén Comte Bertrand Clauzel
> 6e Division – Gén Eugène Casimir Villatte, Comte d'Oultremont
> Brigade St Pol
> Brigade Lamorandière

> 8e Division – Gén Comte Jean Isidore Harispe
> Brigade Dauture   strength   1970
> 9e Léger
> 25e Léger
> 34e Léger

Brigade Baurot strength 2585
10e de Ligne
45e de Ligne
81e de Ligne
115e de Ligne
116e de Ligne
117e de Ligne (-)

La Division de Réserve – Gén Baron Jean-Pierre Travot

Conscrits

Detached

3e Division (Gen Abbé) at Bayonne

7e and 9e Division and 2e Cavalerie Division withdrawn by Napoleon and redeployed to north-eastern France in January 1814

APPENDIX C

Proclamations

From time to time, both Wellington and Soult needed to communicate their instructions to the local French population at large. The method adopted for this type of broadcast was the issue of 'Proclamations' usually in poster form.

In Chapter 1, reference is made to Wellington's Proclamation No. 28 which outlines the responsibilities of Mayors to meet army requisitions. In Chapter 3, reference is made to Soult's Proclamation exhorting Frenchmen to rally to their Emperor against the English. Overleaf, is the fully translated text of Wellington's Proclamation which was issued from his Headquarters at St Lys on 1st April and only a few days before the Battle of Toulouse. Typically, a Proclamation poster such as illustrated here would be posted at the Town Hall (*Mairie*) as well as at other public buildings in the *Département* and communes.

(No. 31.)

PROCLAMATION.

Par Le Feld Maréchal MARQUIS DE WELLINGTON,

Commandant en Chef les Armées Alliées, &c. &c. &c.

AU QUARTIER GENERAL, ce 1 Avril 1814.

1.° Les Maires, ayant sous leurs Ordres les Gardes Communales, sont responsables au Commandant en Chef pour la tranquillité de leurs Communes respectives, et ils feront des-armer tous ceux, qui leur seront suspects de l'intention de l'interrompre.

2.° Le Commandant en Chef fait sçavoir aux habitans du pays, que les loix de la Guerre ne permettent pas, que l'habitant demeurant dans son Village, fasse en même temps le metier de Soldat.

Il faut que ceux, qui desirent être Soldats, aillent servir dans les Rangs Ennemis: et que ceux, qui desirent vivre tranquillement chez eux, sous la protection du Commandant en Chef, ne portent pas les Armes.

3.° Le Commandant en Chef ne permettra à qui que ce soit, de faire les deux metiers; et tout personne, pas Militaire, qui sera trouvé en Armes sur les derrières de l'Armée (ex-cepté ceux dans les Gardes Communales employés sous les Ordres du Maire de la Com-mune par la permission du Commandant en Chef, enoncée de la manière dite en sa Pro-clamation du 23 Fevrier, No. 18,) sera jugé selon les Loix militaires, et traité de la manière qu'ont traité les Generaux Ennemis, les Espagnols et les Portugais.

4.° Le Commandant en Chef espère que, comme jusqu'a present, la tranquillité pu-blique ne sera pas interrompue; et que la droiture et l'autorité des Magistrats, et le bon sens des Gentilhommes et des Citoyens du Pays, lui aideront à diminuer les maux de la Guerre, malgré les Efforts des malveillans et des interressés à les augmenter: mais il fait sçavoir, que si il vient à être dans le cas de faire avancer des troupes, pour conserver la tranquillité publique sur les derrières de l'Armée, les frais de l'entretien et subsistance de telles troupes seront à la charge du district, qui les aura rendu necessaire.

WELLINGTON, &c.

Wellington's Proclamation (No.31)
Courtesy of Les Archives Municipales de Tarbes.

(No. 31)

PROCLAMATION

by Field Marshal Marquess of Wellington

Commander-in-Chief of the Allied Forces, &c. &c. &c.

FROM ARMY HEADQUARTERS 1ˢᵗ April 1814

1 – The Mayors, who have under their command the local guards, are responsible to the Commander-in-Chief for keeping peace in their respective communes. Any persons suspected of breaking the peace are to be disarmed.

2 – The Commander-in-Chief would make known to the inhabitants of the country that, according to the Laws of War, nobody living in the villages is to take up arms. Thus, those who wish to take up arms, should ally themselves on the side of the enemy and those who wish to live peacefully, under the protection of the Commander-in-Chief, should not carry arms.

3 – The Commander-in-Chief forbids any person to carry out both functions. Any non-military person found bearing arms clandestinely (except those in the Guard under the orders of the Mayor and with permission of the Commander-in-Chief as proclaimed on 23ʳᵈ February, No 18) will be judged according to Martial Law and treated in the same manner as they have treated their common enemies, the Spanish and Portuguese.

4 – The Commander-in-Chief trusts that the General Peace will be maintained as has been the case up to the present time; that the rectitude and the authority of the magistrates and the good sense of the citizens will assist him in lessening the ills of War, despite efforts by the trouble-makers and those who aid and abet them. However, it must also be made known that, should it be necessary to send troops to keep the General Peace once the Army has passed through, the costs of support and maintenance of said troops will be borne by the District.

Wellington, &c

The Campaign Memorial at Biarritz

In the porch of the deconsecrated Anglican church of Saint Andrew in Rue Broquedis, Biarritz (now the Musée Historique de Biarritz), there is a magnificent memorial dedicated to the memory of the officers, non-commissioned officers, and men of the British Army who fell in South West France from the 7th October 1813 to the 14th April 1814.

Biarritz is a town on the Atlantic coast a few kilometres south-west of Bayonne. There is no particular or military significance in the Memorial being at Biarritz. However, the town was a favourite resort for the fashionable British in the latter half of the 19th Century and a sizeable English speaking community had established itself in the town. The Biarritz Anglican Church was, therefore, a most appropriate site for the Memorial.

This impressive memorial lists every officer by name and by regiment who died during the campaign in France and gives the place and date of death. On the panel dedicated to those of the 95th Rifles, Captain Duncan is recorded as dying from wounds at Tarbes on the 20th March 1814. NCO and rank & file deaths are also recorded but not as named individuals. For the 20th March 1814, one NCO and five rank & file deaths are listed on the 95th Rifles panel.

The memorial was erected by 'their fellow soldiers and compatriots' in 1882. It was visited by Queen Victoria on the 30th March 1889 and by Edward VII on the 11th March 1906. The memorial is now generally overlooked although it is kept in immaculate condition by the Musée Historique. For those who choose to visit, it is a reminder of the sacrifice made by so many. It is also a remarkable source of research material not found elsewhere.

```
           NINETY  FIFTH  FOOT
              [RIFLE  CORPS]
   CAPT GIBBONS,    D.O.W.   BIDASSOA OCT. 7.
   LT ALEXR CAMPBELL,        BIDASSOA OCT. 7.
   LT JOHN HILL,             BIDASSOA OCT. 7.
   LT JOHN DOYLE, D.O.W.     NIVELLE NOV. 10.
   LT JOHN HOPWOOD,          NIVE DEC. 10.
   CAPT J. DUNCAN, D.O.W.    TARBES MAR. 20.
   N.C.O.— II OCT. 7.— II NOV. 10.
   N.C.O.— I DEC. 10.— I MAR. 20.
   BUGLER.— I NOV. 10.
   R.F.XXVII OCT. 7.— V NOV. 9.
   R.F.— III NOV. 10.— IX DEC. 10.
   R.F.— V MAR. 20.— XVII APL. 10.
```

95th Rifles Memorial Panel – Biarritz.
Courtesy of Le Musée Historique, Biarritz.

95th Rifles Monthly Strength Returns 1814

Illustrated in this Appendix is the consolidated 'Monthly Return of the Strength of the Three Battalions 95th Rifle Regiment, so long as employed in the S. of France during the year 1814'.

Essentially the document is self-explanatory. It illustrates, however, the meticulous nature of regimental administration especially during a relatively fast moving campaign. It covers the period January to June 1814; a six-month period which included the Battle of Orthez, the action at Aire, the combat at Tarbes, and the Battle of Toulouse.

The 'Return' was completed on the 25th of each month and on that date the 'Station' of the three 95th battalions was recorded. On the 25th March 1814, for example, the Regiment is shown to be deployed around L'Isle-en-Dodon en route to Toulouse. After the cessation of hostilities in April 1814, the battalions are shown to be billeted in the area of Castelsarrasin down the River Garonne some 30 kilometers north-west of Toulouse. Here the battalions stayed until ordered to march to their port of embarkation at Bordeaux. The 95th Rifles set off on 1st June and arrived some two weeks later having marched via Lectoure and Condom. At Bordeaux, the battalions encamped near Blanquefort just to the north of the city prior to being called forward for embarkation on 8th July 1814. It is interesting to note that during this period after hostilities had ceased, there were a significant number of deaths and an increase in desertions.

MONTHLY RETURN OF THE STRENGTH OF THE [*Three Batalion Br. Ena. Regiment... 1°S./ Fra*] DURING THE YEAR 1814.

Date	Bt.	Station	Lieut.-Colonels	Majors	Captains	Lieutenants	Ensigns	Paymaster	Adjutant	Quarter-Master	Surgeon	Assistant-Surgeons	Sergeants	Trumpeters, Drummers or Buglers	Present Fit for duty	Sick	On Command	Recruiting	On Furlough	Total	Joined	Transfers Received	Transfers Given	Discharged	Dead	Deserted	Sent Home	Prisoners of War	Remarks
Jany 25	1st	Arrocunka	1	1	5	14	2	1		1	1	2	40 15		446 100	11			557	3		1		3				
	2d	Jala		1	5	10	1	1	1	1	1	2	44 10	356 226	10			572	3	1			4				
	3d	Arrocunka		1	5	18	1	1		1	1	1	30 9	380 139	17			536	1			2	1	2		1	
Feby 25	1	Ustecira	1	1	5	17	2	1	1	1	1	2	39 15	434 84	8			536	1				2	1			
	2	New Orthes	1	1	5	10	2	1	1	1	1	2	44 10	384 91	9			584	1			2	8	1	2		
	3	Camp r Brvn		1	5	19	1	1	1	1	1	1	30 9	373 150	8			531					2		3		
Mar 25	1	St Jean de Luz	1	1	6	17	2	1		1	1	2	40 21	402 93	17			512	1				23	1			
	2d	Espaen		1	4	9	3	1	1	1	1	2	41 15	387 147	46			580	66			1	70	1			
	3d	La Haye		1	5	13	2	1		1	1	1	32 11	354 150	31			575	33				48				
April 25	1	Castel Sarasin	1	1	6	17	2	1		1	1	2	40 15	407 87	16			570					2				
	2d	Castelnan	1	1	4	10	2	1		1	1	2	21 11	364 137	38			563					13				
	3d	Gruzalles		1	5	13	1	1		1	1	1	26 8	315 148	25			489					17	1	12		
May 25	1	Castel Sarasin	2	1	4	16	3	1		1	1	2	41 15	473 61	12			562	57	1			2				
	2d	Gentelnan		1	5	10	4	1		1	1	2	41 11	425 116	38			559	1		1		13	1	2		
	3d	Grugelles			4	14	3	1		1	1	1	25 8	367 110	22			499	21	1			17				
June 25	1	Camp	2	1	4	16	3	1		1	1	2	41 15	473 61	10			544	8	1	1	20	2	1			
	2d		1	1	4	10	4	1		1	1	2	41 11	442 113	22			555	1	1		15	4		2		
	3d	Blang for E	1		4	14	3	1		1	1	1	26 8	373 92	9			474	1				10	6	1		

Battalion strengths remain remarkably stable throughout the period bearing in mind the losses incurred by the Regiment at Orthez, Tarbes, and Toulouse. The 'Return' illustrates that battlefield casualties were being replaced as needed. In the 'Remarks' column an interesting note appears for the return submitted on the 25th March, i.e. just five days after the battle at Tarbes.

'No of men who could not be found in the General Hospital and therefore Struck off as Dead on 25th March, 1814:

1st Battalion   21 rank and file

2nd Battalion   2 Sergeants and 65 rank and file

3rd Battalion   1 Bugler and 44 rank and file.

Total   2 Sergeants, 1 Bugler, 130 rank and file'

The 95th Rifles dead for the battle at Tarbes are shown in Chapter V to be one officer, one sergeant, and five rank and file. The additional 133 men 'struck off as dead' on this Strength Return are assumed to be dead because they could not be found in the General Hospital. This assumption was necessary for regimental administrative reasons and it could be that some were indeed dead. Others could be wounded and cared for by French civilians, while some might be prisoners, stragglers, or deserters. The truth will never be known.

Tarbes – A Battlefield Tour

Maps:

The following Institut Geographique Nationale (IGN) maps are recommended and can be obtained locally in France from most good bookshops and *maisons de la presse*. Town plans of Tarbes can also be obtained locally.

The full IGN map catalogue is shown on the IGN website **www.ign.fr** All IGN maps, including those listed here, can be ordered online from the IGN website.

Map A – Area Coverage

The following area map covers the whole of the Tarbes battle area on one sheet and is suitable for those wishing to drive the route:
   IGN Carte Topographique Série Top 100, 1:100,000 (1cm = 1km)
   Sheet 70   Pau, Bagnères-de-Luchon

Map B – Detailed Coverage

For those wishing to walk at least part of the route, the action on the 20th March 1814 is covered by six map sheets in the:
   IGN Série Bleue (GPS Compatible) 1:25,000 (1cm = 250 m)
   Sheet 1744 O   Vic-en-Bigorre
   Sheet 1744 E   Miélan

Sheet 1745 O	Tarbes
Sheet 1745 E	Montastruc (Hautes-Pyrénées)
Sheet 1746 O	Bagnères-de-Bigorre
Sheet 1746 E	Tournay – Capvern

For those wishing to concentrate only on the 95th Rifles action on the Orleix ridge, Sheet 1745 O Tarbes is recommended.

Should anyone wish a more authentic approach to the tour, the appropriate sheets of the 18th Century 1:86,400 'Carte de Cassini' may also be obtained from IGN.

Map C – Town Plan of Tarbes

INTRODUCTION

The modern *Régions* of Aquitaine and Midi-Pyrénées (formerly the Provinces of Guyenne, Gascogne and Béarn) abound with sites of interest for those who wish to follow in the footsteps of Wellington's and Soult's armies as they lumbered from the Atlantic coast to Toulouse.

The modern administrative *Départements* of Pyrénées-Atlantiques (64), Landes (40), Gers (32), and Hautes-Pyrénées (65) are remarkably unchanged since 1813-1814. Undeniably, cities and towns have expanded and urbanisation has claimed some battlefield sites as, for example, at Toulouse. In general, however, most sites are easily identifiable.

San Sebastian, the Bidassoa estuary, the Pyrenees, Bayonne, Orthez, Tarbes, and Toulouse are all within striking distance of each other on good uncrowded roads. Additionally, there are various places of interest to visit including the Guards' cemeteries at Bayonne and the Memorial at Biarritz. To sustain the battlefield tourist, local Gascon dishes such as *foie gras, confit,* and *magret de canard* and regional wines make this area particularly special.

This Appendix proposes a route through the battle area by concentrating on the fortunes of the 95th Rifles and their progress on the 19th and 20th March 1814.

THE 95TH RIFLES TRAIL

Haget (Map A).   It was in and around this small village some 4 kms north of Rabastens, that the 95th Rifles bivouacked on the night of the 19th March after a long day's march from Plaisance via Auriébat. Next morning, the 95th were up and about by 3.15am and, marching in the dark, moved along the D280/D124 to Rabastens.

Rabastens (Map A).   At Rabastens, Beresford's Column assembled before dawn and at approximately 7.30am on the 20th March, the Column moved off towards Tarbes heading south along *'La Grande Route de Tarbes à Rabastens'*, now the *Route Nationale 21 (N21)*. Notice how the ridges develop on the left.

Orleix (Map B Sheet 1745 O)   At approximately 12.5 kms south of Rabastens on the N21, there is a turning on the left to Orleix. It was near this point that the leading elements of the Column spotted the French. What appeared at first to be a small piquet was seen on the crest of the nearest ridge and the 95th Rifles were dispatched to deal with it not knowing that Harispe's 8th Division was deployed on and behind the ridge. At the same time, Clinton's 6th Division, which was further down the Column, was ordered to leave the main road and deploy east through Dours, then on to Sabalos on the Oléac ridge in the hope of manoeuvring behind the French. The Oléac ridge can readily be seen from the Orleix turning and the old telegraph tower is clearly visible on the crest. Turn off the N21 into Orleix and take the single track road which runs south between the N21 and the ridge down to Bois-Sibal.

Orleix Ridge (Map B Sheet 1745 O)   It was in the area Bois-Sibal that the 95th Rifles' action started. The three battalions skirmished onto the ridge leading up to Point 352. Note the Canal d'Alaric which Simmons described as 'a small river in front of the position'. Retrace the route back to Orleix and now take the road/track running along the eastern edge of the ridge. Walk up to Point 352. From this vantage point there is a fine view of Tarbes set against the Pyrenees illustrating that Soult had no escape route to the south. It is possible to discern the route which Hill's Column took from Vic-en-Bigorre and the general course of the River Adour. To the east, the Oléac to Boulin ridge is clearly defined. It was to this ridge that Harispe's 8th Division retreated across the flat 'plain', while Clinton's 6th Division closed on Boulin from the area of the tower, driving Villatte's Division off the high ground.

Points 352 and 354 (Map B Sheet 1745 O)   The protracted skirmishing executed by the 95th Rifles culminated in a 'sharp' firefight with Harispe's heavy infantry in the general area around Points 352 and 354. As Harispe's men withdrew, they moved east to Boulin. It is worth taking the single track road across the flat ground and up to Boulin.

Boulin (Map B Sheet 1745 O)   Once on the Oléac to Boulin ridge, look back to the Orleix ridge to appreciate how well Harispe's and Villatte's men were deployed. Move through Boulin and head back towards Tarbes on the D632. After approximately 1km turn left onto the D49 to Souyeaux. It was in this direction that the Light Division and the 95th Rifles pursued the retreating French. At Souyeaux join the D5 and head south. It was between the D5 and the River l'Arrêt that the Light Division came to rest on the evening of the 20th March. The French had taken up positions on the Lhez ridge and the 95th Rifles were close enough to the ridge to be 'cannonaded' (the Lac de l'Arrête darré is a modern man-made lake). The 6th Division came to rest in the area of Coussan.

Lhez Ridge (Map B Sheet 1745 E)   Continue south on the D5 and where it joins the N117 turn eastwards. Go through Lhez onto the ridge and look back over the ground. It is here worth reflecting on the day of the action. The 95th Rifles had started that morning at 3am, marched many kilometres, fought a hard battle and pursued the enemy. At 6.30pm they came to rest but even then patrols were deployed. Reflect also on the brilliant use of ground by the French. The Lhez ridge was the perfect position from which to execute a night withdrawal.

Return to Tarbes (Map B Sheets 1745 O and 1746 O)   At Lhez, rejoin N117 and head towards Tarbes retracing in reverse the advance of Hill from Tarbes and Soult's retreat. At Piétat, notice the steepness of the hill and imagine both armies with their artillery, equipment, and wounded struggling to the top.

Tarbes (Map B Sheet 1745 O)   Continue along the N117 to its junction with the D632 Boulin road. Due west from this is the bridge that the French and then Hill debouched from Tarbes; the bridge which the French failed to demolish (the existing bridge is modern).

Tarbes Centre (Map C)   Most of the old buildings in Tarbes have long since disappeared. Comte Péré's house where both Soult and then Wellington lodged has been demolished but the imposing gate through which they rode can still be seen where Rue Georges Magnoac joins Rue Massey. The Cathedral still stands as does the 18th Century Hôpital de l'Ayguerote adjacent to it. Here the wounded were treated and in a temporary military hospital close by. From Tarbes centre, leave on the D935 and head north towards Vic-en-Bigorre.

The Adour Valley (Maps A and B Sheet 1745 O)   Travelling north on the D935, the ridge to the west can be seen rising from the valley. It was here, on the night of the 19th March, that Reille's and Clauzel's Corps came to rest in the area of Ger. After leaving Tarbes, there is a road (D2) which leads to Bours where 'red-coated officers of the English Army' watched the battle from the church tower as it unfolded. Follow the D935 into Andrest and on to the village of Pujo around which D'Erlon's Corps took up positions after being driven out of Vic-en-Bigorre by Picton's 3rd Division on the 19th.

Vic-en-Bigorre (Map A)   On the morning of the 20th March, Vic-en-Bigorre was the assembly point for the Allied Right Column before it set off south under General Sir Rowland Hill towards Tarbes. In the vineyards to the north of Vic on the 19th, General Picton with the 3rd Division and, in support, Clinton's 6th Division and Bock's Cavalry Brigade, drove D'Erlon's rear-guard through and beyond Vic.

Summary.   There are many permutations to the route suggested above. Fortunately the terrain has changed little and it is relatively easy to imagine the two great armies on the move in their columns. Tens of thousands of men and horses, followed by trains of baggage, equipment, artillery, and wounded, and then by camp followers, descended onto this hitherto quiet corner of France. Tarbes was a small country town in 1814 of no great political or strategic importance. Its inhabitants enjoyed rural tranquillity and were not greatly involved in their Emperor's successes and failures. Yet on the 19th and 20th March 1814, their peace was shattered as first the French and then the Allied armies passed through the area. This suggested tour seeks merely to remind us of those dramatic events.

Selected Bibliography

Anton, James. *Retrospect of a Military Life During the Most Eventful Periods of the Last War* Edinburgh 1841

Batcave, Louis. *La Bataille d'Orthez 27 Février 1814.* Imprimerie Lescher–Montoué, Pau 1914

Batty, Capt. *Campaign of the Left Wing of the Allied Army in the Western Pyrenees and the South of France in the years 1813-1814* Murray, London 1823

Beatson, Maj Gen F.C. *Wellington. The Crossing of the Gaves and the Battle of Orthez.* Heath Cranton, London 1925

Blakiston, John. *Twelve Years' Military Adventure in Three Quarters of the Globe* Vol II 1829

Butler, Lewis. *Wellington's Operations in the Peninsula* Vol II, Fisher Unwin, London 1904

Cameron, Alexander. *Letters* collected in the Rifle Brigade Chronicle 1931

Carme-Duplan. *Précis Historique de la bataille livrée le 10 Avril 1814 sous les Mures de Toulouse* Toulouse 1815

Chandler, David. *A Dictionary of the Napoleonic Wars* Arms and Armour Press, London 1979

Claye, Léonce, Baron de. Unpublished MS *'Souvenirs de Famille'* 1876 in the possession of the Marquis de Verthamon

Clerc, Le Commandant du 49ème d'infanterie. *Campagne du Maréchal Soult dans les Pyrénées Occidental en 1813-1814* Librairie militaire de L. Baudoin, Paris 1894

Cooke, Capt. J.H. *Memoirs of the Late War Vol II The Personal Narrative of Captain Cooke of the 43rd Regiment* Colburn and Bentley, London 1831

Cope, Sir William. *The History of the Rifle Brigade* Chatto & Windus, London 1877

Costello, Edward. *Adventures of a Soldier* Longmans, Green, London 1852

Cox, William. Notes taken from unpublished MS Journal of William Cox, Willoughby Verner, Rifle Brigade Archive

Croker, John W. *The Croker Papers Vol III* ed. L. Jennings, London 1884

Daniel, J.E. *Journal of an Officer in the Commissariat Department of the Army* London 1820

Debofle, Pierre. *La Retraite de l'Armée d'Espagne et son Passage par les confins du Gers en 1814* Société Archéologique et Historique du Gers, Troisième Trimestre 1991

Dumas, Lt Col Jean-Baptiste. *Neuf Mois de Campagne à la suite du Maréchal Soult* Editions Henri Charles-Lavauzelle, 1907

Escalettes, Jean Paul. *10 Avril 1814, La Bataille de Toulouse* Edns. Loubatières 1999

Frazer, Augustus. *Letters of Colonel Sir Augustus Frazer* ed. E. Sabine, Naval and Military Press, London 2001

Fry, Mary and Davies, Godfrey. *Sir Charles Alten* Journal of The Society of Army Historical Research Vol 33

Gates, David. *The British Light Infantry Arm 1790-1815* Batsford, London 1987

Gairdner, James. Unpublished MS Diaries of Lt James Pensman Gairdner, National Army Museum, London

Germain, Pierre. *Drouet d'Erlon* Éditions F. Lanore, F. Sorlot Éd, Paris 1985

Gibaud, Pascal. *Un Village – Orleix*

Glover, Michael. *The Peninsular War 1807-14 A Concise Military History* Penguin, London 2001
Wellington's Army in the Peninsula 1808-14 David and Charles, London 1977

Green, William. *A Brief Outline of the Travels and Adventures of William Green* Coventry 1857

Griffith, Paddy. ed. *Wellington – Commander: The Iron Duke's Generalship* Antony Bird, London 1985

Hardinge, Richard. *Letters from the Peninsula 1812-1814* Part II ed. M. Laws in the Royal Artillery Journal 1959

Harispe, Général Comte Jean Isidore. Unpublished MS letter dated 24 October 1813 in the possession of Michael Ayrton

Harris, Rifleman. *Recollections of Rifleman Harris* ed. H Curling 1848

Harvey, Basil. *The Rifle Brigade* Leo Cooper, London 1975

Hayman, Sir Peter. *Soult. Napoleon's Maligned Marshal* Arms and Armour Press, London 1990

HQ of the Army. *General Regulations and Orders for the Army* Adjutant General's Office, Horse Guards 1811
General Orders Volume 6 '1814 France' London 1817

Hill, Sir Rowland. *The Hill Papers,* British Library.

Hulot, Frédéric. *Le Maréchal Soult* Pygmalion 2003

Kincaid, John. *Adventures in the Rifle Brigade* London, Boone 1830
Random Shots from a Rifleman 1835

Larpent, Sir George. *The Private Journal of Judge-Advocate Larpent* (3rd Edition 1854) Reprint 2000 with an introduction by Ian C. Robertson, Spellmount, London 2000

Larronde, Claude. *Soult dans les Pyrénées* Société Académique des Hautes-Pyrénées 2000
Soult et Wellington dans les Pyrénées 1813-1814 Princi Negue 2004

Lawrence, William. *Autobiography* Sampson Low, Marston, Searle and Rivington. London 1886

Leach, Jonathan. *Rough Sketches of the Life of an Old Soldier* Longman, Rees, Orme, Brown and Green, London 1831

Leslie, Charles. *A Treatise on the Employment of Light Troops on Actual Service* William Clowes, London 1843

Leslie, NB. *Battle Honours of the British and Indian Armies 1695-1914* Leo Cooper, London 1970

Light Division. *Standing Orders ... for the Light Division 1809-11* ed. Campell and Shaw. Government Printing Office.

Longford, Elizabeth. *Wellington. The Years of the Sword* Weidenfeld & Nicholson, London 1969

Malcolm, John. *Reminiscences of a Campaign in the Pyrenees and South of France in 1814* in *Constable's Miscellany xxviii Memorials of the Late War* Vol I, Constable, Edinburgh 1828

Martinien, A. *Tableaux Des Officiers Tués et Blessés 1805-1815* Éditions Militaires Européennes, Paris 1899

Massie, Colonel. *A Propos de l'Affaire de Tarbes du 20 Mars 1814* Bulletin de la Société Académique des Hautes-Pyrénées 1953

Meyricke, John. MS. Unpublished letters in the possession of his descendant, Rory Constant

Ministère de la Guerre. MS. Documents sur la Campagne d'Espagne de 1811-1814 demandé pour le Colonel Napier 1833. National Army Museum, London

Moore Smith, GC. *The Life of John Colborne, FM Lord Seaton* Murray, London 1903

Muir, Rory. *Tactics and the Experience of Battle in the Age of Napoleon* Yale, London 1988

Myatt, Frederick. *Peninsular War General, Sir Thomas Picton 1758-1815* David & Charles, London 1980

Napier, Sir William. *A History of the War in the Peninsula and in the South of France 1807-1814* Warne, London 1892

Norman, CB. *Battle Honours of the British Army* John Murray, London 1911

Oman, Sir Charles. *A History of the Peninsular War* Vol VII Clarendon 1930 and Vol IX ed. P. Griffith, Greenhill, London 1999

Page, FCG. *Following the Drum: Women in Wellington's Wars* Deutsch, London 1986

Peyrouzet. *La Campagne de 1814 dans les Hautes-Pyrénées* Revue des Hautes-Pyrénées, Février 1939

Picton, Sir Thomas. *Memoirs of Lt Gen Sir Thomas Picton* ed. HB Robinson, Richard Bentley, London 1836

Powell, A. *The Barnard Letters* 1928

Revue de Gascogne. *Bulletin Mensuel de la Société Historique de Gascogne* Tome XXIX Auch 1888

Rifle Brigade. *Standing Regulations for the Rifle Brigade* London 1819

Robertson, Ian C. *Wellington Invades France. The Final Phase of the Peninsular War 1813-1814* Greenhill Books, London 2003

Robinson, CW. *Wellington's Campaigns* Vol 3 1813-15

Robinson, RER. *The Bloody Eleventh. History of the Devonshire Regiment* Vol I, Exeter 1988

Ross-Lewin, Harry. *With the Thirty-Second in the Peninsula and other Campaigns* ed. J. Wardell, Dublin 1904

Rottenburg, Colonel. *Regulations for the Exercise of Riflemen and Light Infantry and Instructions for Their Conduct in the Field* London 1803

Schaumann, August. *On the Road with Wellington* Greenhill 1999

Simmons, George. *A British Rifle Man* ed. W. Verner, A&C Black, London 1899

Smith, Digby. *The Greenhill Napoleonic Wars Data Book 1792-1815* Greenhill Books, London 1998

Smith, Sir Harry. *The Autobiography of Lt Gen Sir Harry Smith* ed. GC Moore Smith, Murray, London 1902

Southey, Robert. *History of the Peninsular War* Volume III. London 1832

Surtees, William. *Twenty-Five Years in the Rifle Brigade* Muller, London 1973

Teffeteller, Gordon. *The Surpriser: The Life of Rowland, Lord Hill* Associated University Presses, London 1983

Wellington, Duke of. *Dispatches of FM Duke of Wellington* Vol XI ed. J Gurwood, John Murray, London 1838

Selections from the Dispatches and General Orders of FM Duke of Wellington ed. J Gurwood, John Murray, London 1851

Supplementary Dispatches, Correspondence, and Memoranda of FM Duke of Wellington Vol XIV ed. by his son, John Murray, London 1872

References

I The Pursuit into France.
1. Harispe.
2. Claye.
3. Hill, Additional Manuscripts 35.061 .
4. Frazer p. 449.
5. Ministère de la Guerre, Doc No 60.
6. Larronde 2004 p. 87.
7. Lawrence p. 176.
8. Ross-Lewin p. 234.
9. Ibid.
10. Larronde 2000 p. 76.
11. Debofle p. 305 .

II The Eve of Action.
12. Wellington. Supplementary Dispatches pp. 426-7.
13. Ministère de la Guerre, Doc No 71.
14. Picton pp. 314-5.
15. Cooke pp. 104-5.
16. Ministère de la Guerre, Doc No 72.
17. Massie.
18. Wellington. Dispatches p. 596.
19. Larpent p. 445.
20. Crocker p. 275.

III   French Preparations and Allied Plans for the 20th March.

21   Soult's Proclamation à l'Armée 8 Mars 1814 in Wellington's Dispatches pp. 594-5.
22   Ministère de la Guerre, Doc No 73.
23   Kincaid 1830 p. 143.
24   Letter to Alexander Cameron. Cameron pp. 230-1.
25   Wellington. Supplementary Dispatches pp. 427-8.

IV   Sunday the 20th March – The Allies Engage the French.

26   Cooke p. 106.
27   Kincaid 1830 p. 287.
28   Simmons pp. 343-4.
29   Blakiston p. 343.
30   Ibid.
31   Daniel p. 300.
32   Massie.
33   Simmons p. 343.
34   Surtees p. 286.
35   Costello p. 144.
36   Cope p. 170.
37   Napier p. 147.
38   Blakiston p. 344.
39   Cox p. 6.
40   Costello p. 144.
41   Smith, Harry p. 175.
42   Letter to Alexander Cameron. Cameron pp. 230-1.
43   Malcolm p. 286.
44   Gibaud p. 9.
45   Meyricke.
46   Peyrouzet.
47   Cooke p. 107.
48   Surtees p. 288.

V   The Afternoon of the 20th March – The Pursuit towards Tournay.

49   Robinson, RER p. 510.
50   Surtees p. 288.
51   Simmons p. 344.

52 Blakiston p. 345.
53 Cooke pp. 108-9.
54 Blakiston pp. 345-6.
55 Simmons p. 344.
56 Glover 1977 p. 138.
57 Wellington. Supplementary Dispatches pp. 428-9.
58 Surtees p. 288.
59 Wellington. Supplementary Dispatches p. 429.
60 Gairdner.
61 Hardinge pp. 245-6.
62 Leach pp. 359-361.
63 Blakiston p. 346.
64 Cope p. 171.
65 Martinien pp. 141-467.
66 Ministère de la Guerre, Doc No 73.
67 Wellington. Dispatches pp. 596-7.

VI A Review of Events of the 20th March.

68 Wellington. Dispatches p. 606.
69 Ministère de la Guerre, Doc No 73.
70 Simmons p. 343.
71 Picton p. 316.
72 Blakiston p. 344.

VII Subsequent Events in SW France.

73 Ministère de la Guerre, Doc No 74.
74 Larronde 2000 p. 98.
75 Anton p. 109.
76 Simmons p. 344.
77 Ibid pp. 342-3.
78 Gibaud p. 9.
79 Larpent p. 446.
80 Gairdner.
81 Wellington. Supplementary Dispatches pp. 529-530.
82 Ibid.
83 The Times 8th April 1814.
84 Wellington. Dispatches p. 606.
85 Wellington. Selections p. 803.

86   Simmonds pp. 345-347.
87   Ross-Lewin p. 235.
88   Frazer pp. various.
89   Ibid pp. 447-8.
90   Smith, Harry p. 175.
91   Ibid p. 176-7.
92   Meyricke.
93   Frazer pp. 478-480.
94   Ibid p. 483.
95   Ross-Lewin pp. 236-7.
96   Frazer p. 483.
97   Schaumann pp. 408-9.
98   Ibid pp. 410-1.
99   Longford pp. 347-8.
100   Cited in Harvey p. 38.
101   Blakiston pp. 344-5.

Index

References to illustrations in bold